MYTHOLOGY GRAPHICS

JASON AND THE ARGONAUTS

A MODERN GRAPHIC GREEK MYTH

BY STEPHANIE PETERS

ILLUSTRATED BY LE NHAT VU

CAPSTONE PRESS
a capstone imprint

Published by Capstone Press, an imprint of Capstone
1710 Roe Crest Drive, North Mankato, Minnesota 56003
capstonepub.com

Library of Congress Cataloging-in-Publication Data
Names: Peters, Stephanie True, 1965- author. | Vu, Le Nhat, illustrator.
Title: Jason and the Argonauts : a modern graphic greek myth / by Stephanie Peters ; illustrated by Le Nhat Vu.
Description: North Mankato, Minnesota : Capstone Press, 2024. | Series: Mythology graphics | Includes bibliographical references. | Audience: Ages 9-11 | Audience: Grades 4-6 | Summary: "When young hero Jason sets out to claim his rightful throne, he faces many challenges along the way. The most difficult of all? Capturing the Golden Fleece. Thankfully, he has his fellow heroes—the Argonauts—by his side. Find out if Jason and his pals succeed in their quest in this modern, graphic retelling of a classic Greek myth."— Provided by publisher.
Identifiers: LCCN 2023015203 (print) | LCCN 2023015204 (ebook) | ISBN 9781669059073 (hardcover) | ISBN 9781669059240 (paperback) | ISBN 9781669059257 (pdf) | ISBN 9781669059271 (kindle edition) | ISBN 9781669059264 (epub)
Subjects: LCSH: Argonauts (Greek mythology)—Juvenile literature. Argonauts (Greek mythology)—Comic books, strips, etc. | Mythology, Greek—Juvenile literature. | LCGFT: Mythological comics. | Graphic novels.
Classification: LCC BL820.A8 P48 2024 (print) | LCC BL820.A8 (ebook) | DDC 398.20938/02—dc23/eng/20230417
LC record available at https://lccn.loc.gov/2023015203
LC ebook record available at https://lccn.loc.gov/2023015204

Editorial Credits
Editor: Alison Deering; Designer: Jaime Willems; Production Specialist: Whitney Schaefer

Printed and bound in the USA. PO 5626

TABLE OF CONTENTS

CHAPTER 1

THE HERO WITH ONE SHOE

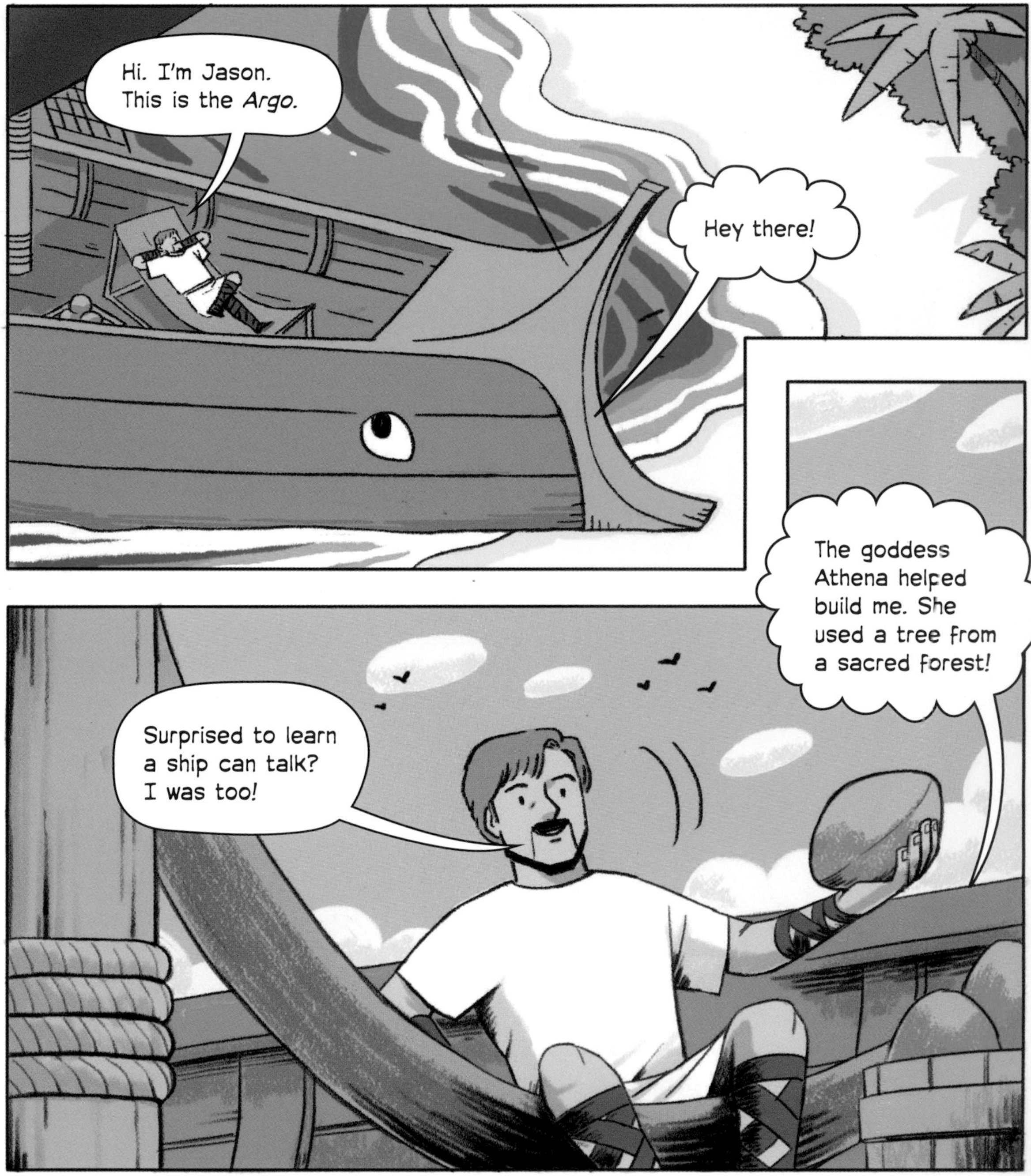

Hi. I'm Jason. This is the *Argo.*
Hey there!
The goddess Athena helped build me. She used a tree from a sacred forest!
Surprised to learn a ship can talk? I was too!

Discovering my ship could talk was just one part of my exciting adventures.

Ooo! Tell the story, Jason! And start from the beginning.

#StoryTime

It all started back when I was a baby. My father was a king. But my uncle Pelias stole his throne.

Take him away.

Uncle Pelias planned to get rid of me too.

Oh, Jason . . . Come out, come out, wherever you are!

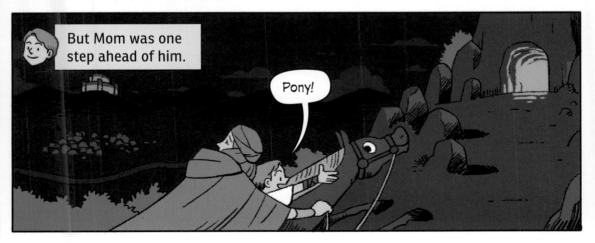

But Mom was one step ahead of him.

Pony!

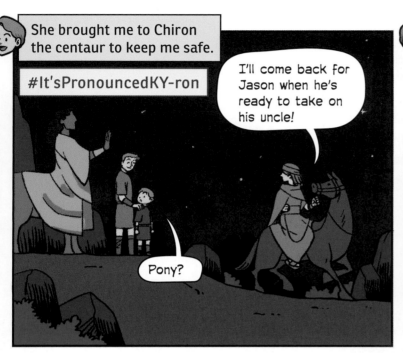

She brought me to Chiron the centaur to keep me safe.

#It'sPronouncedKY-ron

I'll come back for Jason when he's ready to take on his uncle!

Pony?

Chiron coached lots of heroes. He even trained Hercules!

Zeus is my dad. He's king of the gods!

Wow!

#Herc'sMyHero!

Life with the two of them was great. I learned all the important stuff.

Vegetables are good for you.

#CentaurSplaining

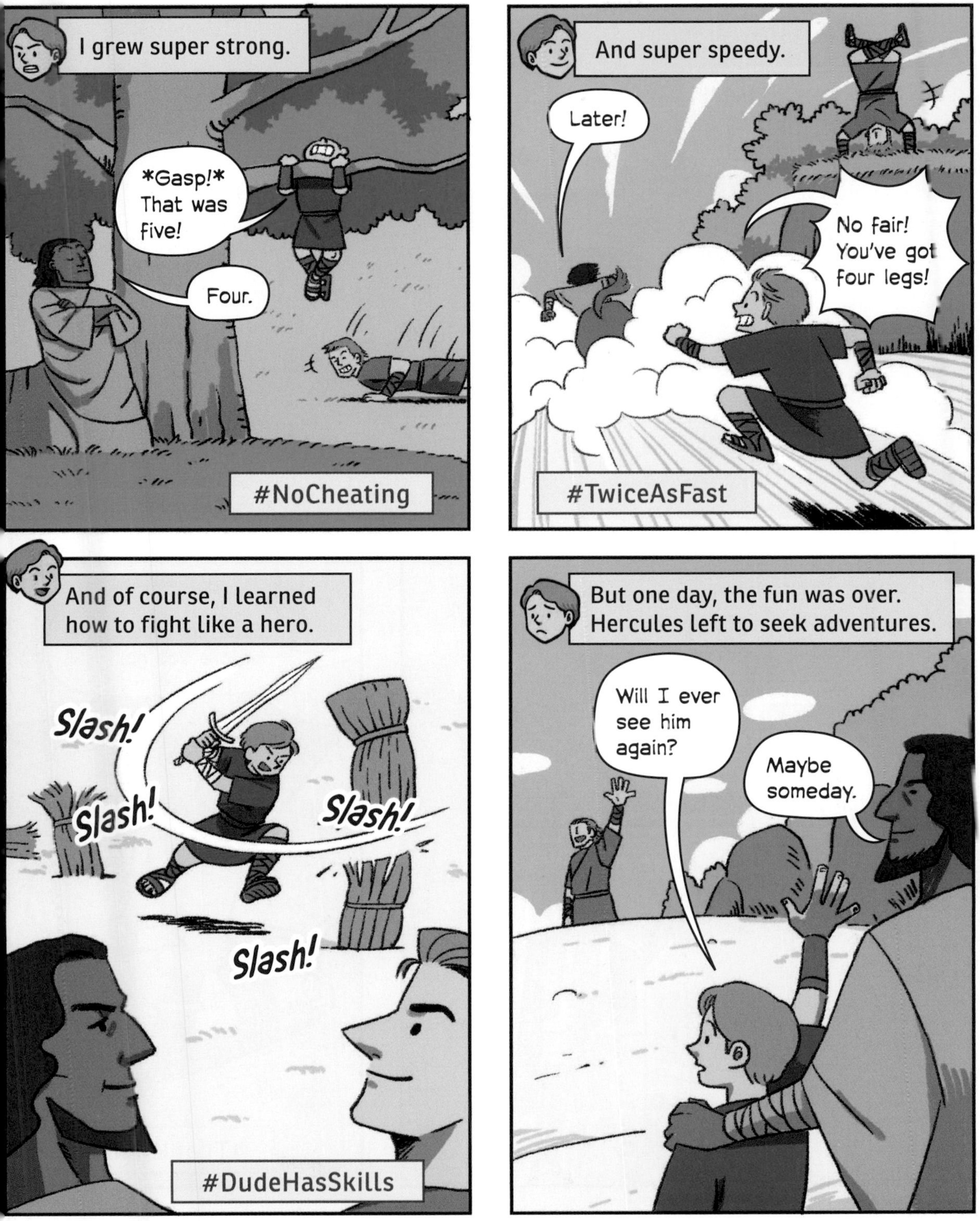
I grew super strong.
Gasp! That was five!
Four.
#NoCheating
And super speedy.
Later!
No fair! You've got four legs!
#TwiceAsFast
And of course, I learned how to fight like a hero.
Slash!
Slash!
Slash!
Slash!
#DudeHasSkills
But one day, the fun was over. Hercules left to seek adventures.
Will I ever see him again?
Maybe someday.

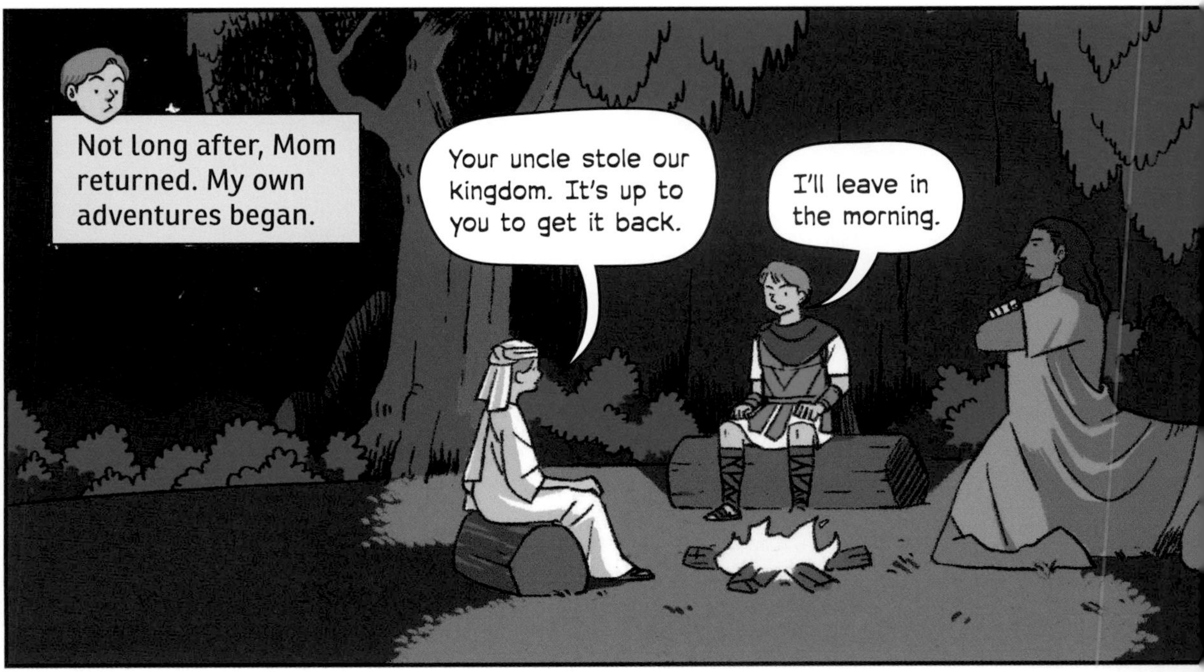
Not long after, Mom returned. My own adventures began.
Your uncle stole our kingdom. It's up to you to get it back.
I'll leave in the morning.

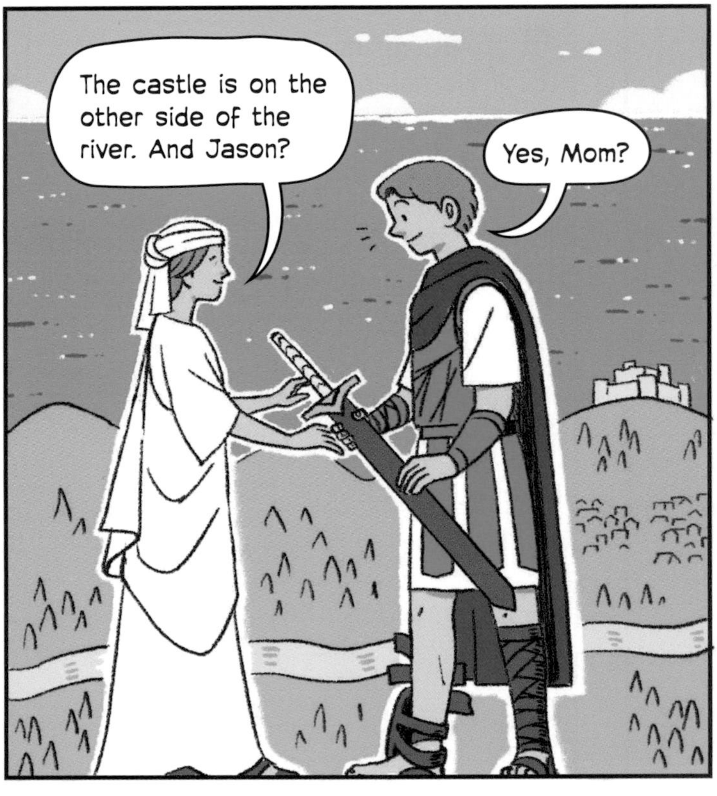
The castle is on the other side of the river. And Jason?
Yes, Mom?

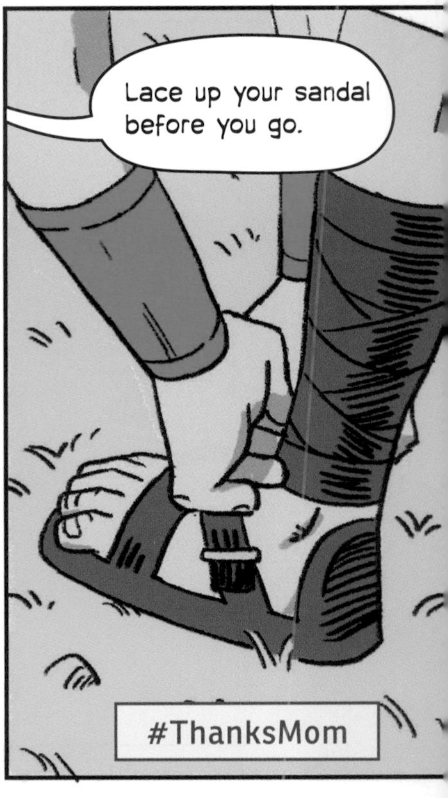
Lace up your sandal before you go.
#ThanksMom

On the way to the river, I ran into an old lady.

Oof!

Whoops! Sorry!

To apologize, I carried her to the other side.

Dang it! I lost a sandal.

splash

#PiggybackRide!

Turns out, it wasn't any old lady. It was Hera, queen of the gods!

Gasp!

As a thank you for your kindness, I'll watch over you from now on.

#HeraOnMyTeam

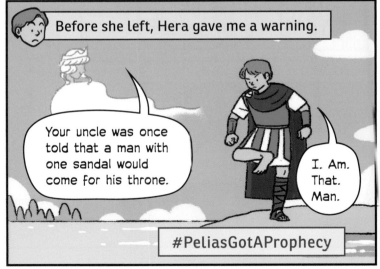

Before she left, Hera gave me a warning.

Your uncle was once told that a man with one sandal would come for his throne.

I. Am. That. Man.

#PeliasGotAProphecy

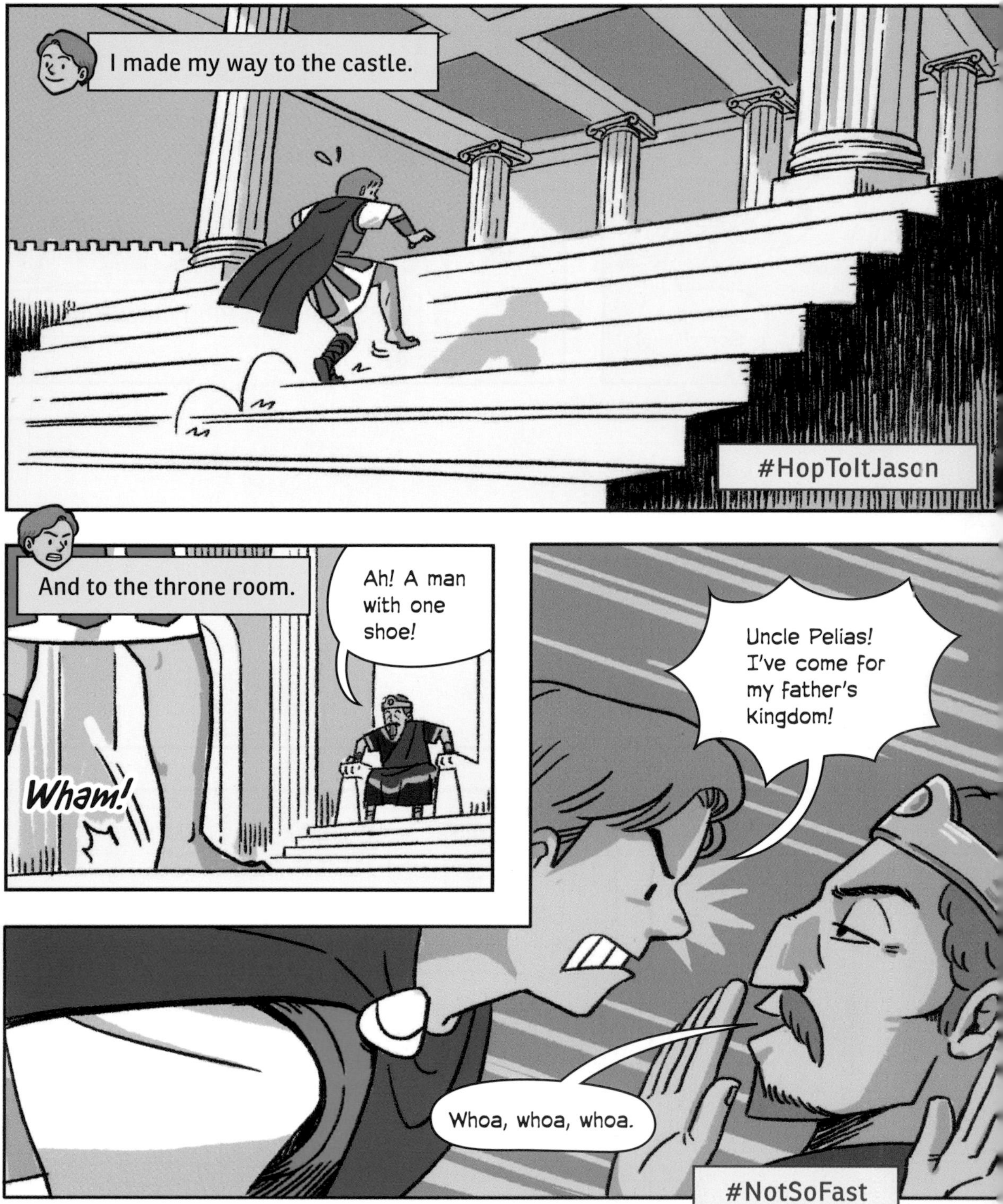
I made my way to the castle.
#HopToItJason
And to the throne room.
Ah! A man with one shoe!
Wham!
Uncle Pelias! I've come for my father's kingdom!
Whoa, whoa, whoa.
#NotSoFast

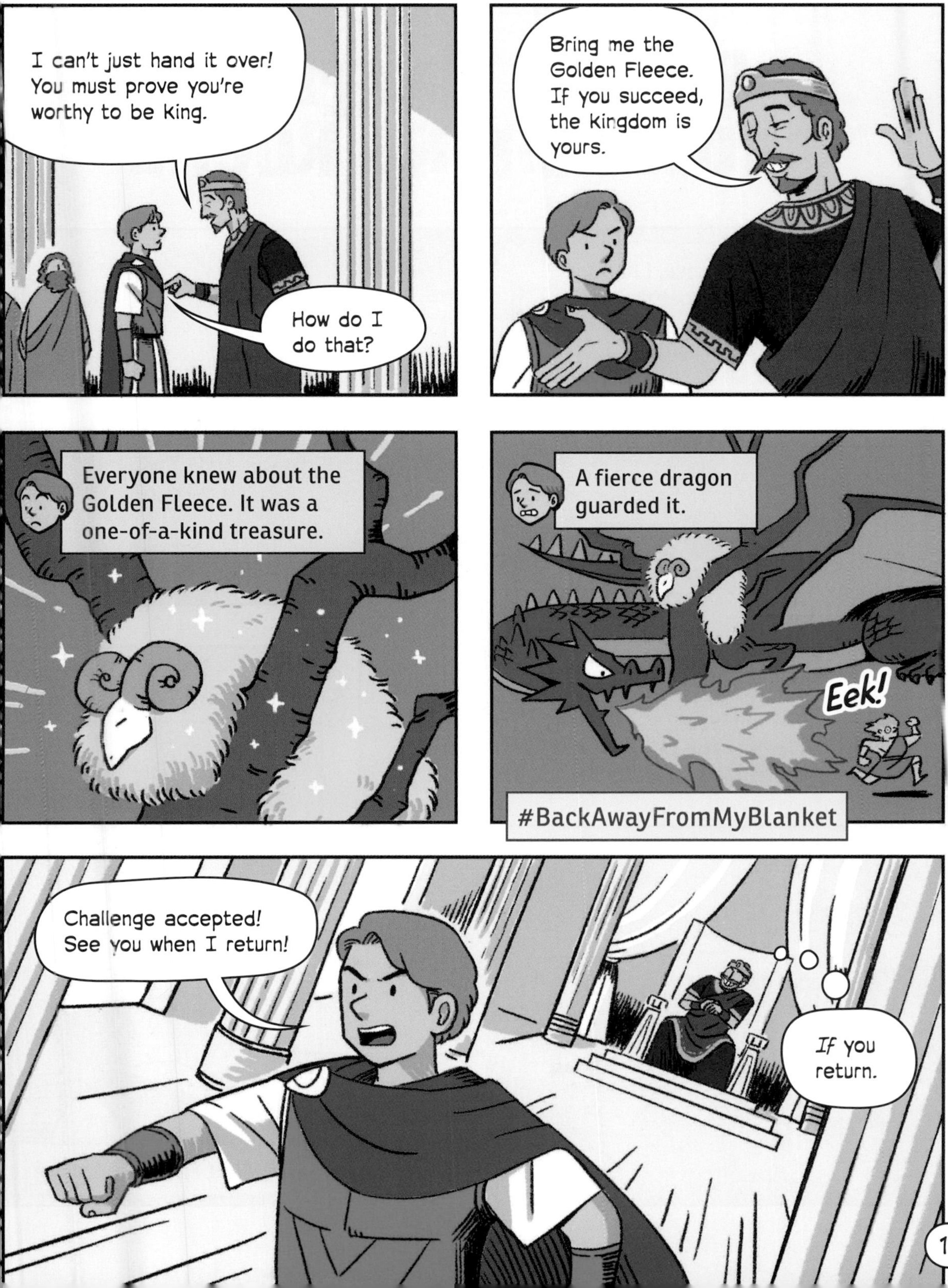
I can't just hand it over! You must prove you're worthy to be king.
How do I do that?
Bring me the Golden Fleece. If you succeed, the kingdom is yours.
Everyone knew about the Golden Fleece. It was a one-of-a-kind treasure.
A fierce dragon guarded it.
Eek!
#BackAwayFromMyBlanket
Challenge accepted! See you when I return!
If you return.

CHAPTER 2

GIANTS, HARPIES, AND CLASHING ROCKS

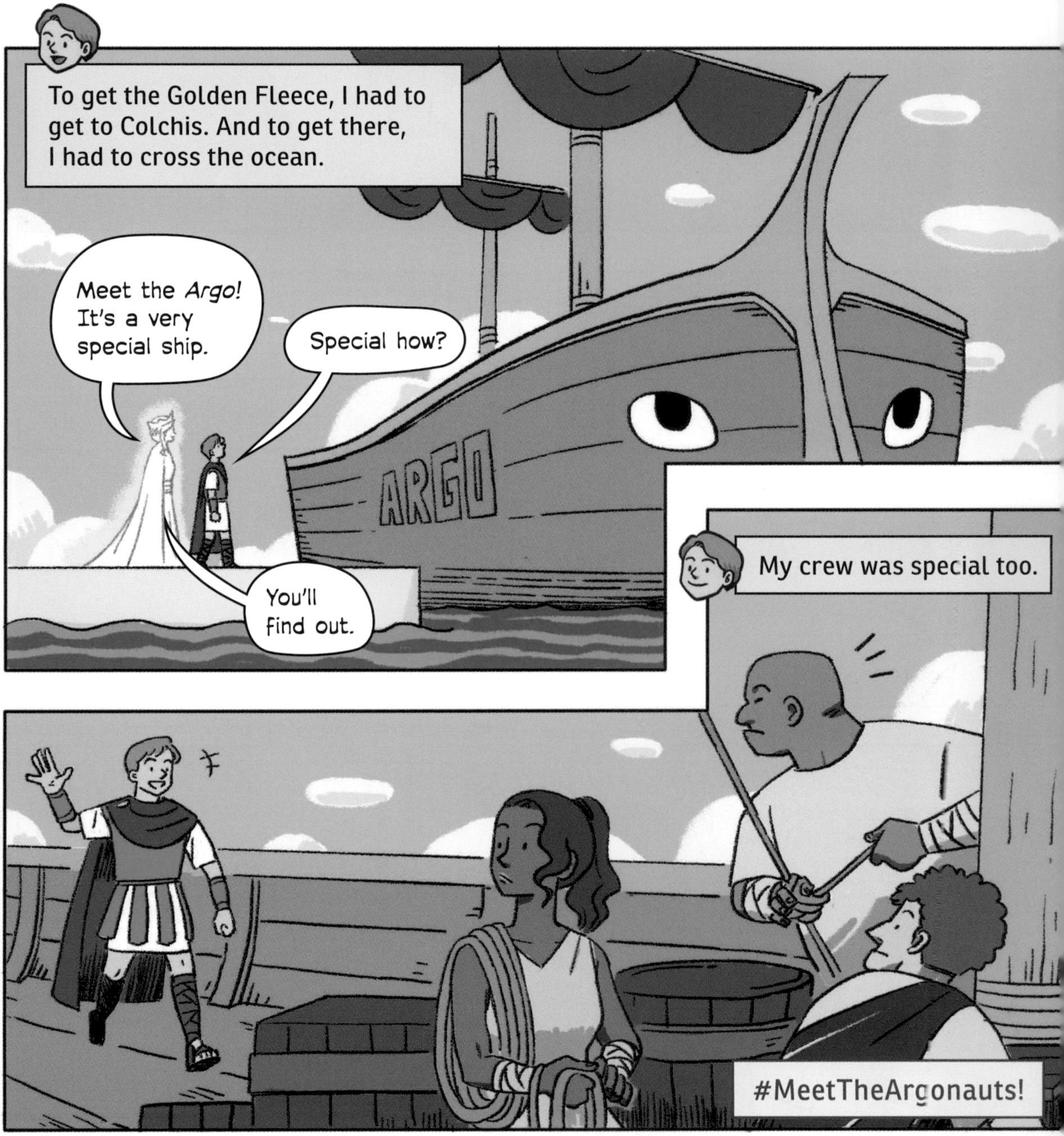
To get the Golden Fleece, I had to get to Colchis. And to get there, I had to cross the ocean.
Meet the *Argo!* It's a very special ship.
Special how?
ARGO
You'll find out.
My crew was special too.
#MeetTheArgonauts!

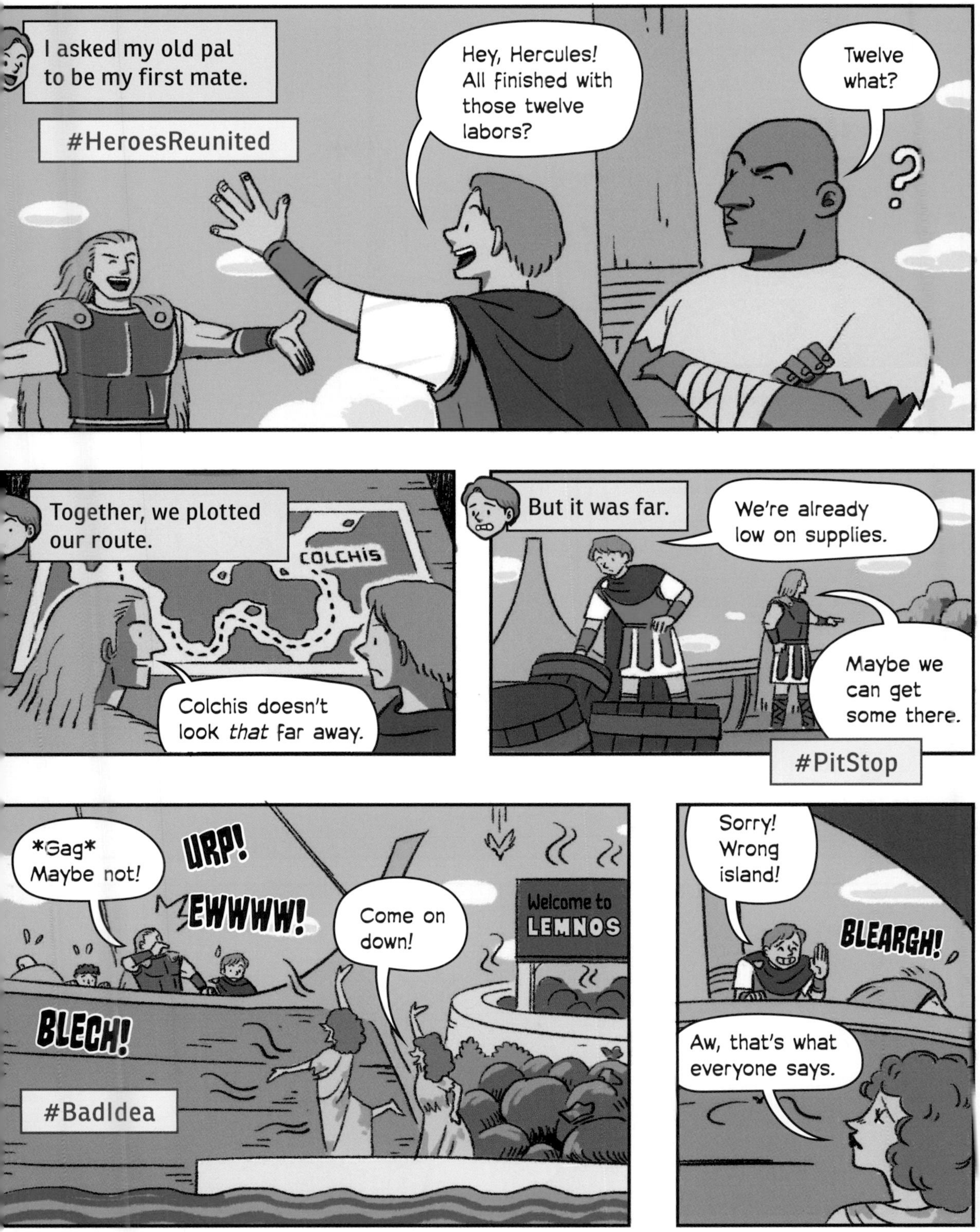
I asked my old pal to be my first mate.
#HeroesReunited
Hey, Hercules! All finished with those twelve labors?
Twelve what?
?
Together, we plotted our route.
COLCHIS
Colchis doesn't look *that* far away.
But it was far.
We're already low on supplies.
Maybe we can get some there.
#PitStop
Gag Maybe not!
URP!
EWWWW!
BLECH!
Come on down!
Welcome to LEMNOS
#BadIdea
Sorry! Wrong island!
BLEARGH!
Aw, that's what everyone says.

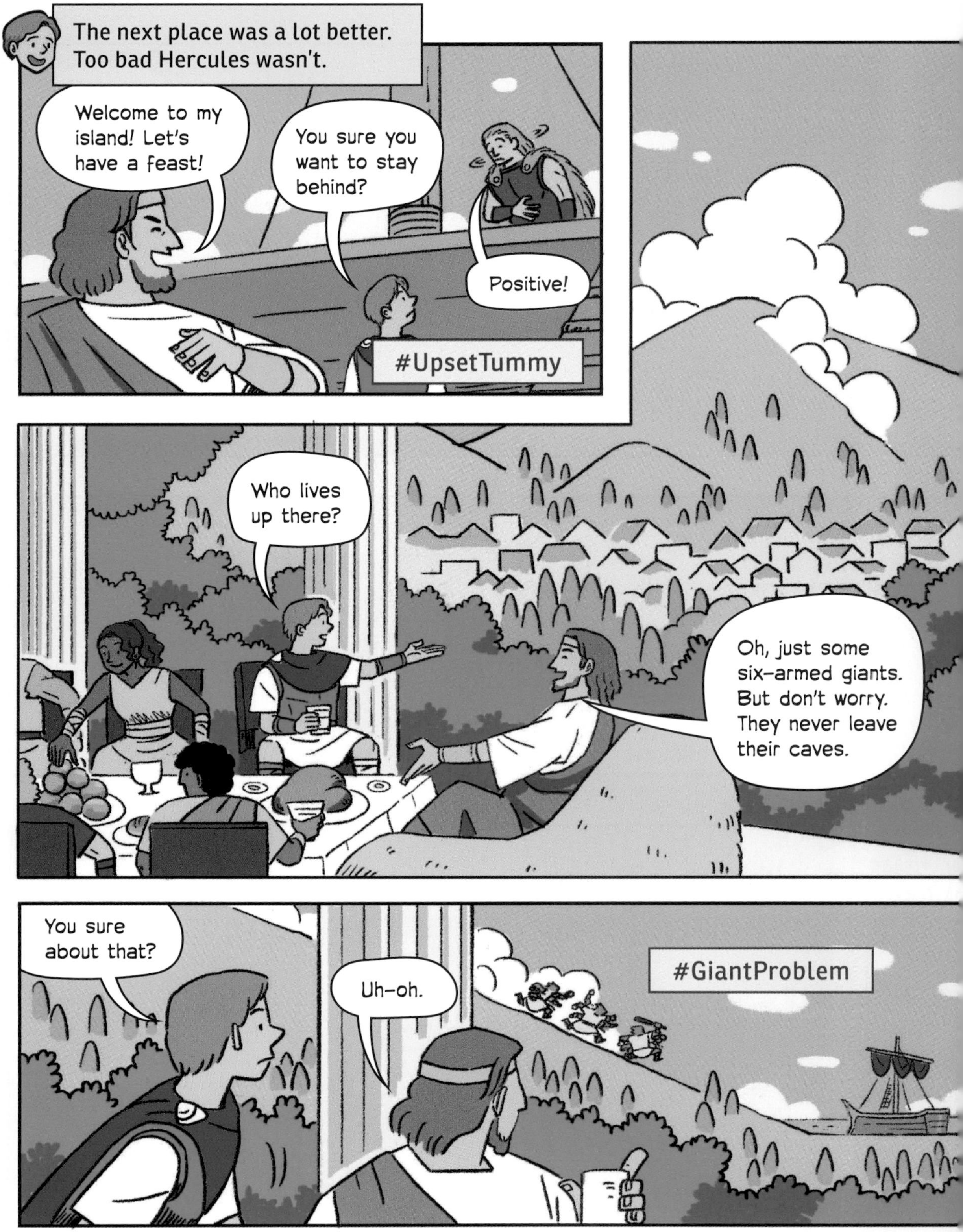
The next place was a lot better. Too bad Hercules wasn't.
Welcome to my island! Let's have a feast!
You sure you want to stay behind?
Positive!
#UpsetTummy
Who lives up there?
Oh, just some six-armed giants. But don't worry. They never leave their caves.
You sure about that?
Uh-oh.
#GiantProblem

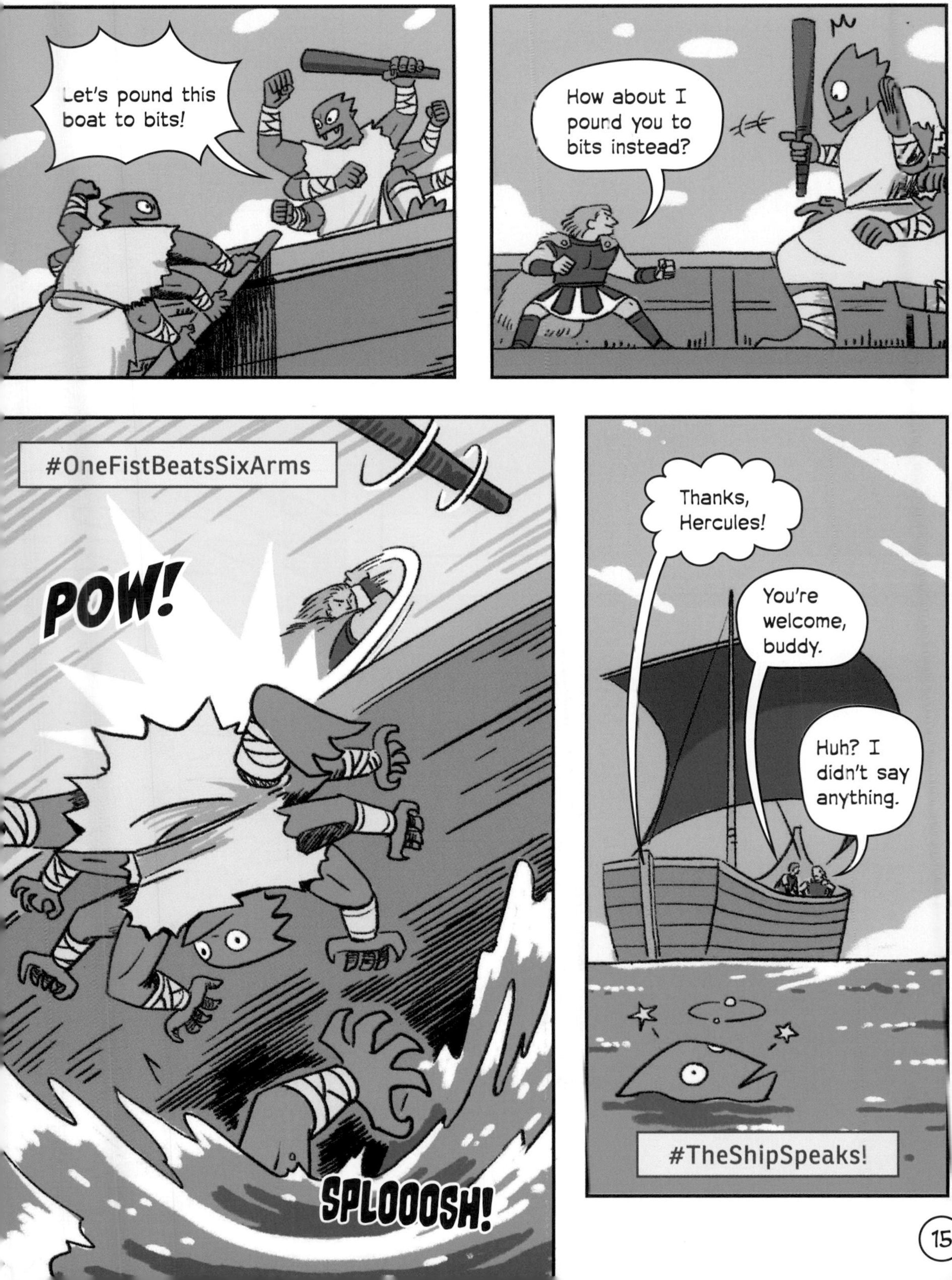
Let's pound this boat to bits!
How about I pound you to bits instead?
#OneFistBeatsSixArms
POW!
SPLOOOSH!
Thanks, Hercules!
You're welcome, buddy.
Huh? I didn't say anything.
#TheShipSpeaks!

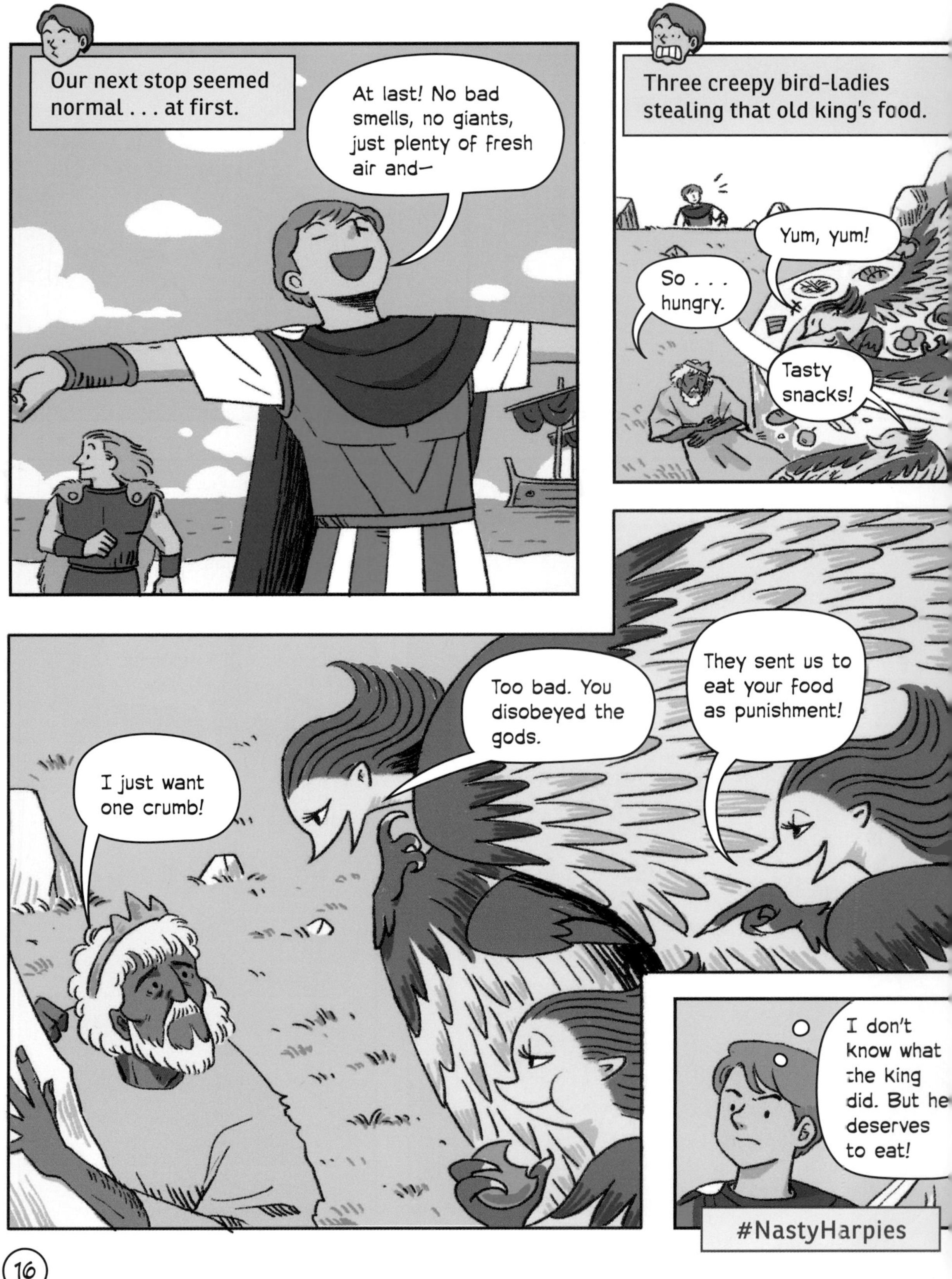
Our next stop seemed normal . . . at first.
At last! No bad smells, no giants, just plenty of fresh air and—
Three creepy bird-ladies stealing that old king's food.
Yum, yum!
So . . . hungry.
Tasty snacks!
I just want one crumb!
Too bad. You disobeyed the gods.
They sent us to eat your food as punishment!
I don't know what the king did. But he deserves to eat!
#NastyHarpies

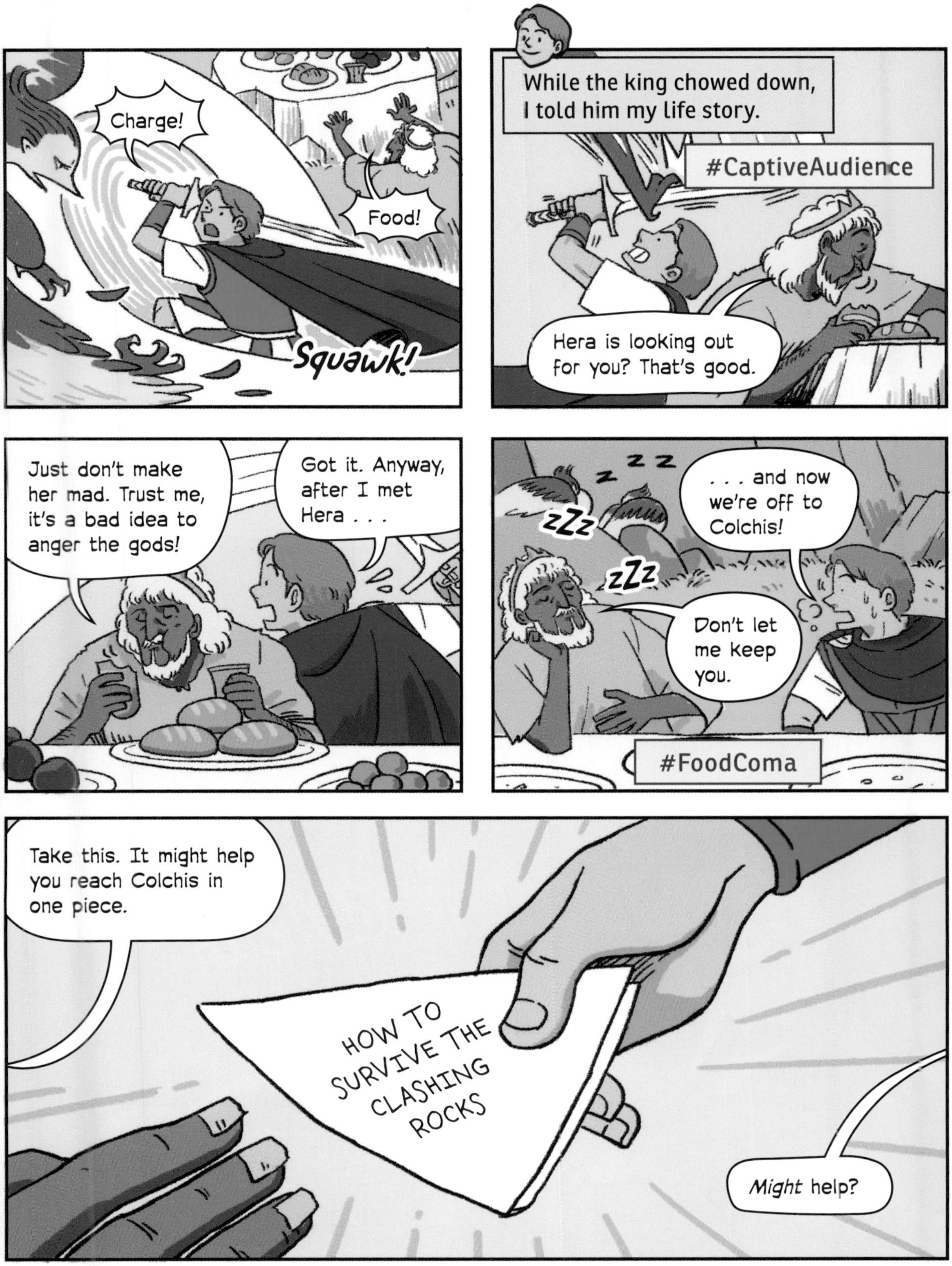

Charge!
Food!
Squawk!
While the king chowed down, I told him my life story.
#CaptiveAudience
Hera is looking out for you? That's good.
Just don't make her mad. Trust me, it's a bad idea to anger the gods!
Got it. Anyway, after I met Hera . . .
Z Z Z
zZz
zZz
. . . and now we're off to Colchis!
Don't let me keep you.
#FoodComa
Take this. It might help you reach Colchis in one piece.
HOW TO SURVIVE THE CLASHING ROCKS
Might help?

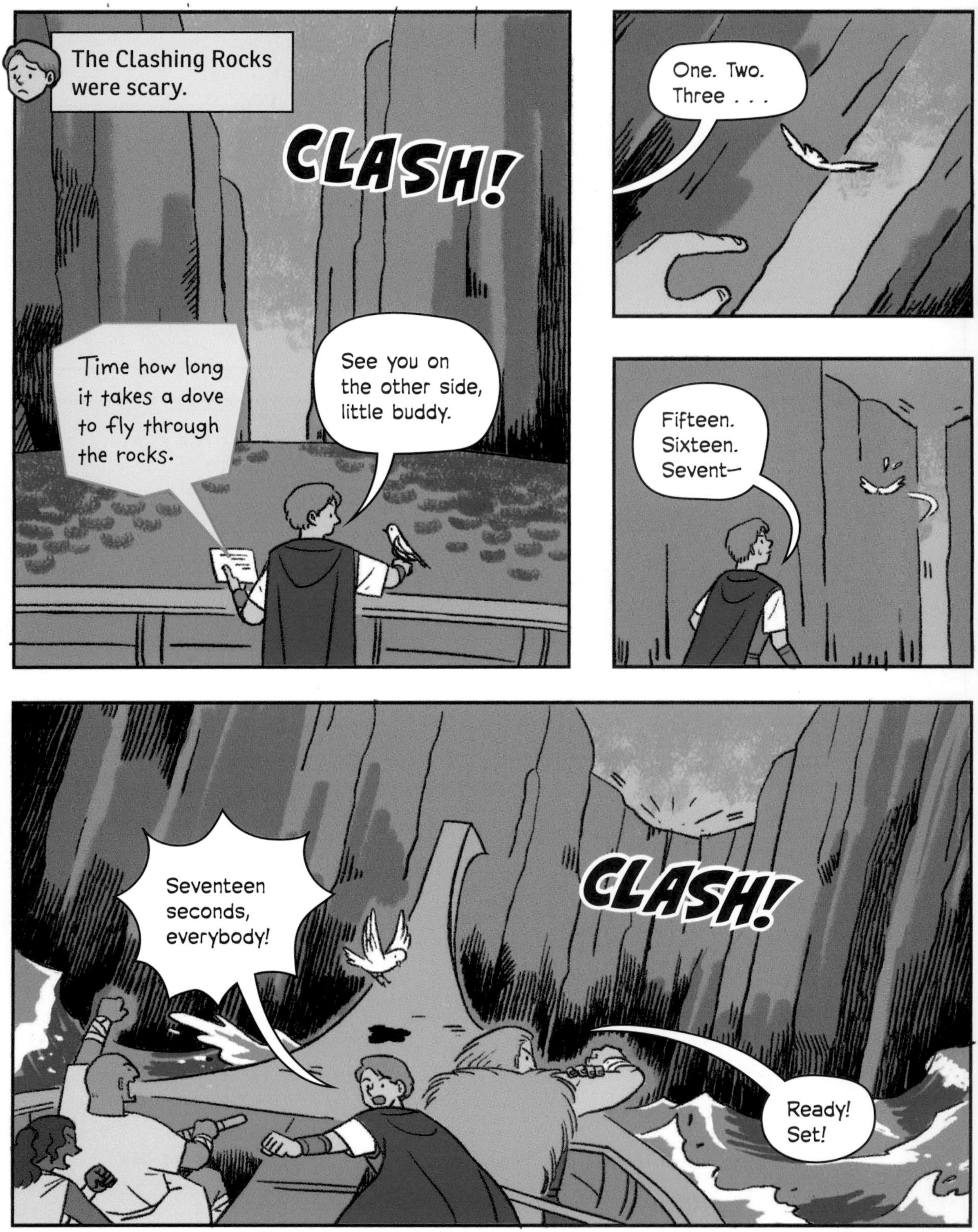
The Clashing Rocks were scary.
CLASH!
Time how long it takes a dove to fly through the rocks.
See you on the other side, little buddy.
One. Two. Three . . .
Fifteen. Sixteen. Sevent—
Seventeen seconds, everybody!
CLASH!
Ready! Set!

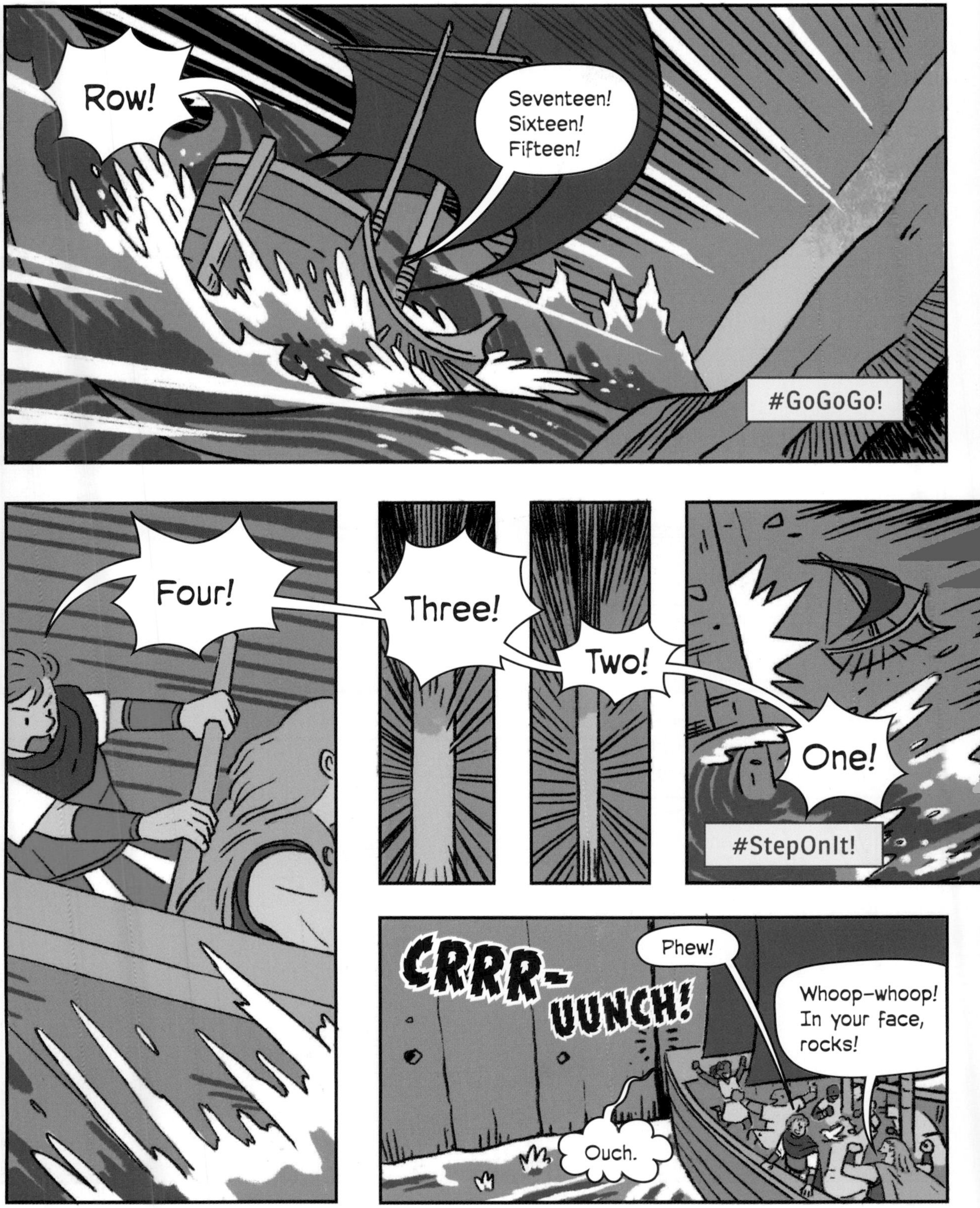
Row!
Seventeen! Sixteen! Fifteen!
#GoGoGo!
Four!
Three!
Two!
One!
#StepOnIt!
CRRR-UUNCH!
Phew!
Whoop-whoop! In your face, rocks!
Ouch.

CHAPTER 3

GET YOUR FLEECE ON!

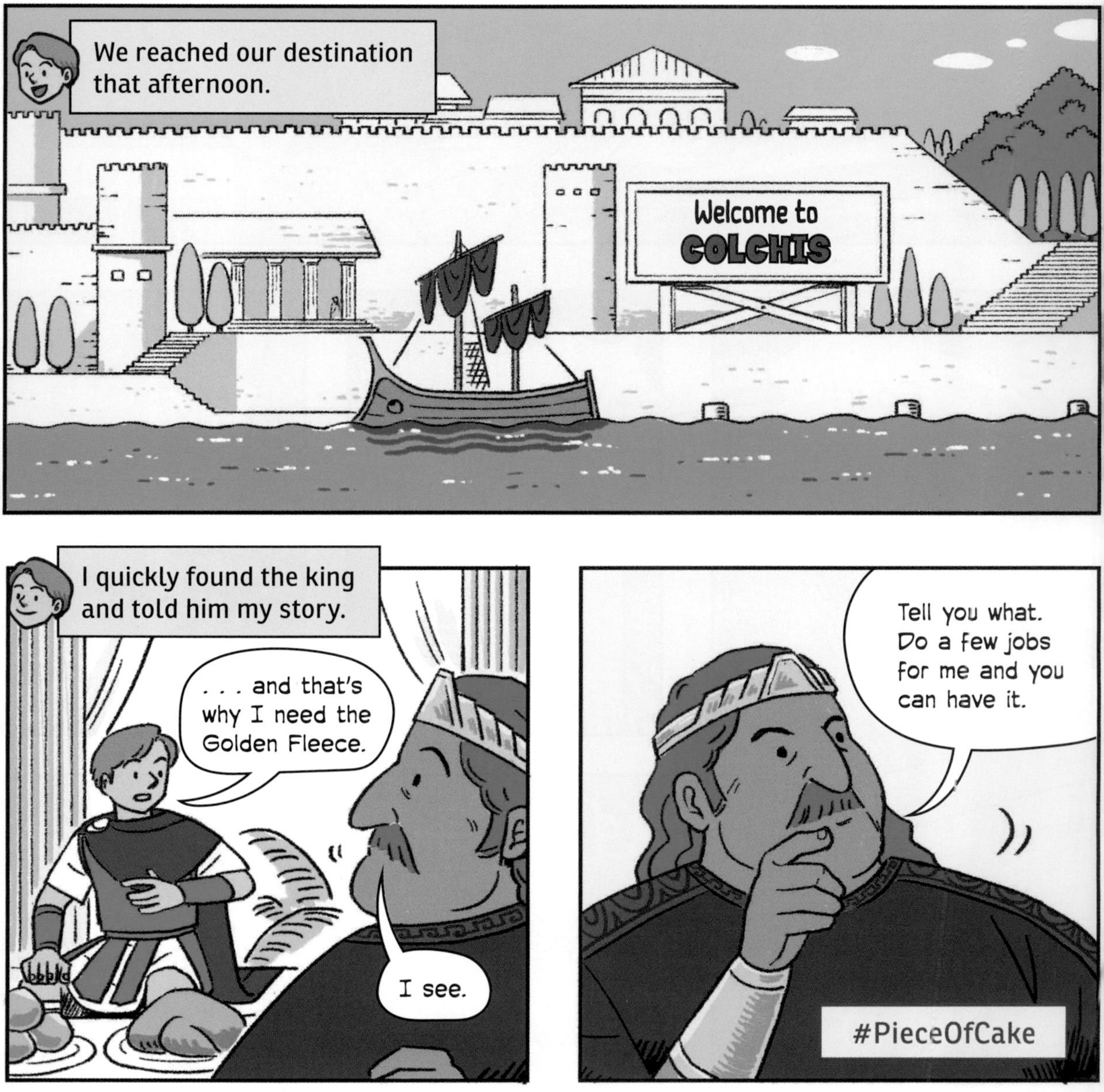
We reached our destination that afternoon.
Welcome to COLCHIS
I quickly found the king and told him my story.
. . . and that's why I need the Golden Fleece.
I see.
Tell you what. Do a few jobs for me and you can have it.
#PieceOfCake

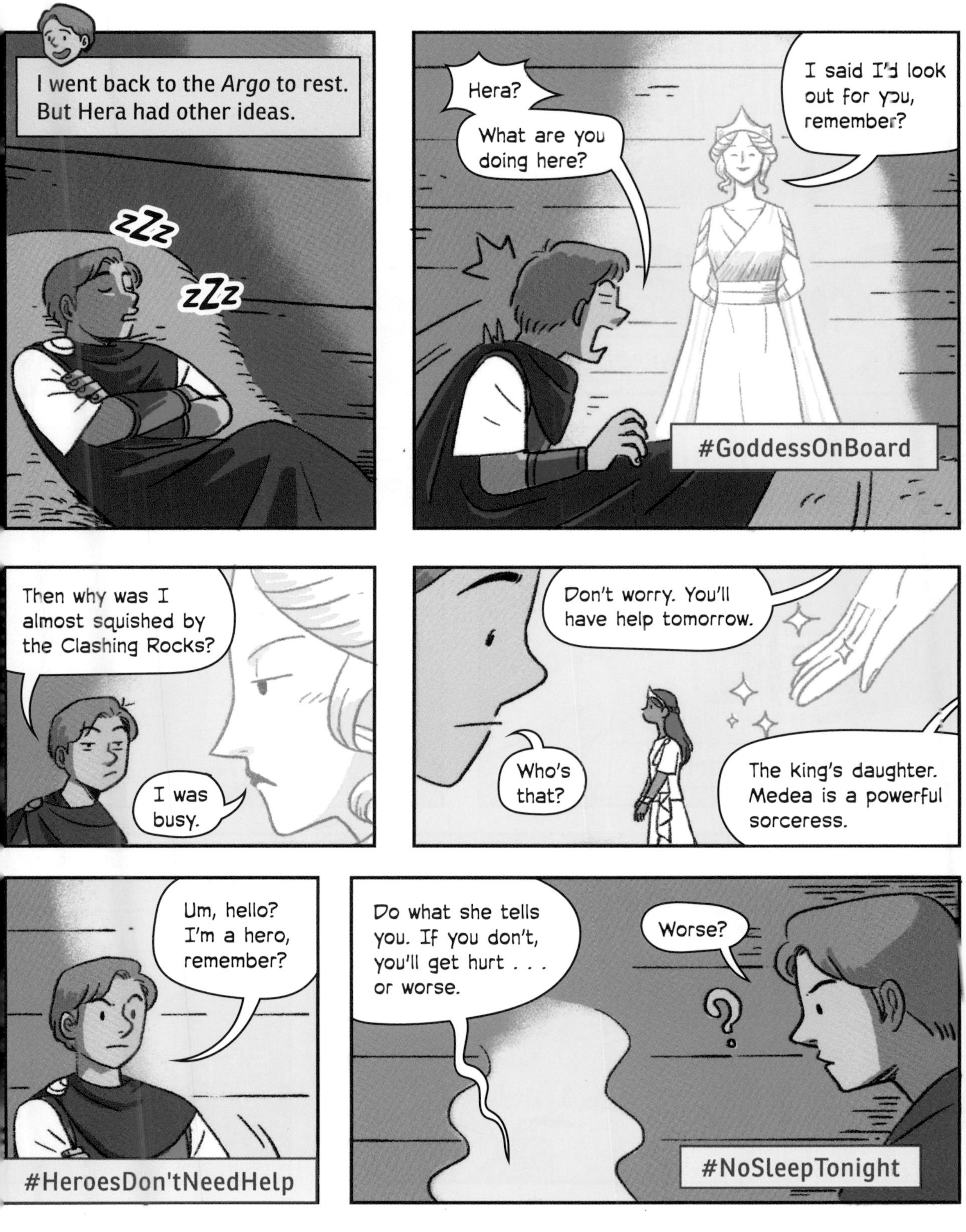
I went back to the *Argo* to rest. But Hera had other ideas.
zZz
zZz
Hera?
What are you doing here?
I said I'd look out for you, remember?
#GoddessOnBoard
Then why was I almost squished by the Clashing Rocks?
I was busy.
Don't worry. You'll have help tomorrow.
Who's that?
The king's daughter. Medea is a powerful sorceress.
Um, hello? I'm a hero, remember?
#HeroesDon'tNeedHelp
Do what she tells you. If you don't, you'll get hurt . . . or worse.
Worse?
?
#NoSleepTonight

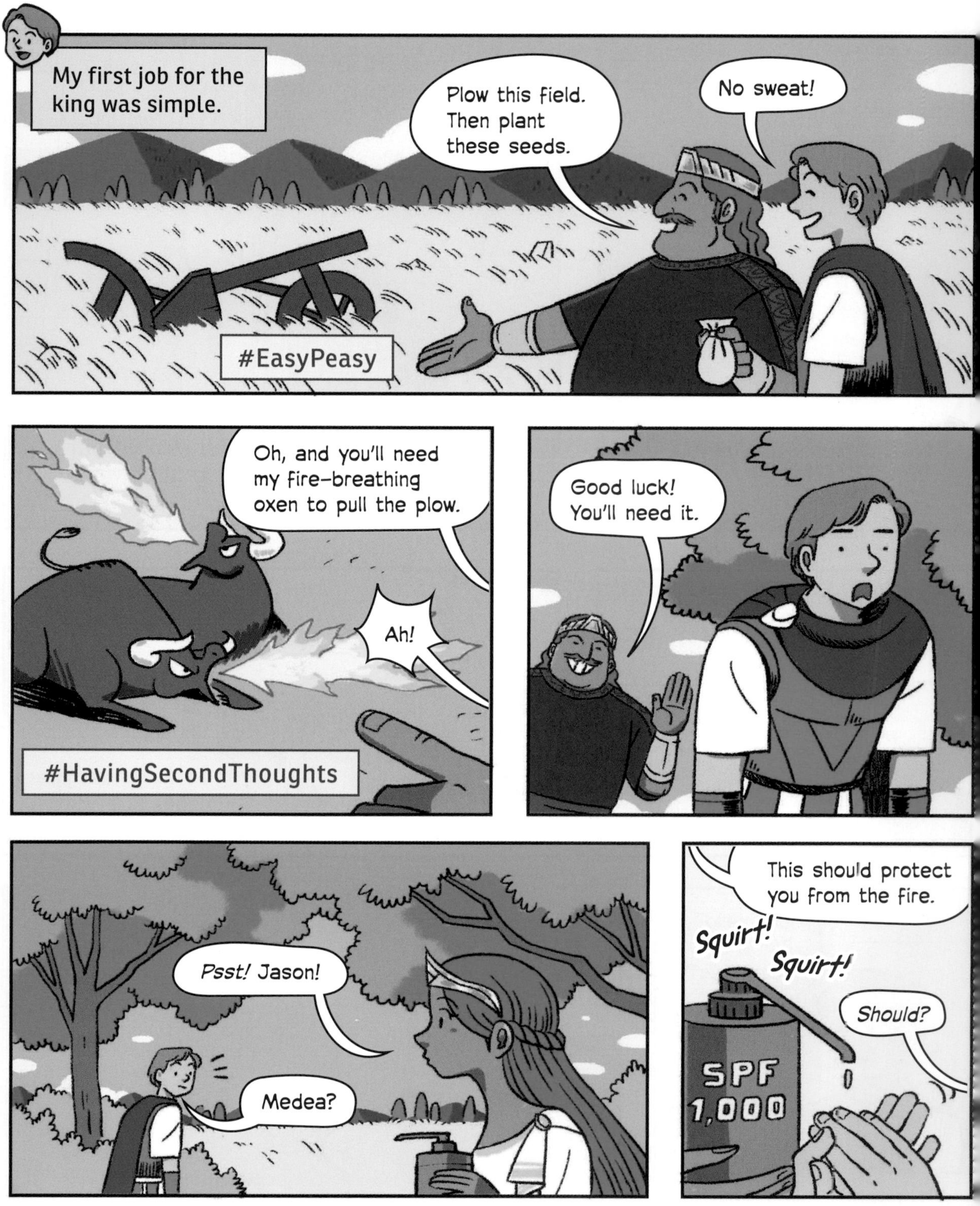

My first job for the king was simple.
Plow this field. Then plant these seeds.
No sweat!
#EasyPeasy
Oh, and you'll need my fire-breathing oxen to pull the plow.
Ah!
#HavingSecondThoughts
Good luck! You'll need it.
Psst! Jason!
Medea?
This should protect you from the fire.
Squirt!
Squirt!
SPF 1,000
Should?

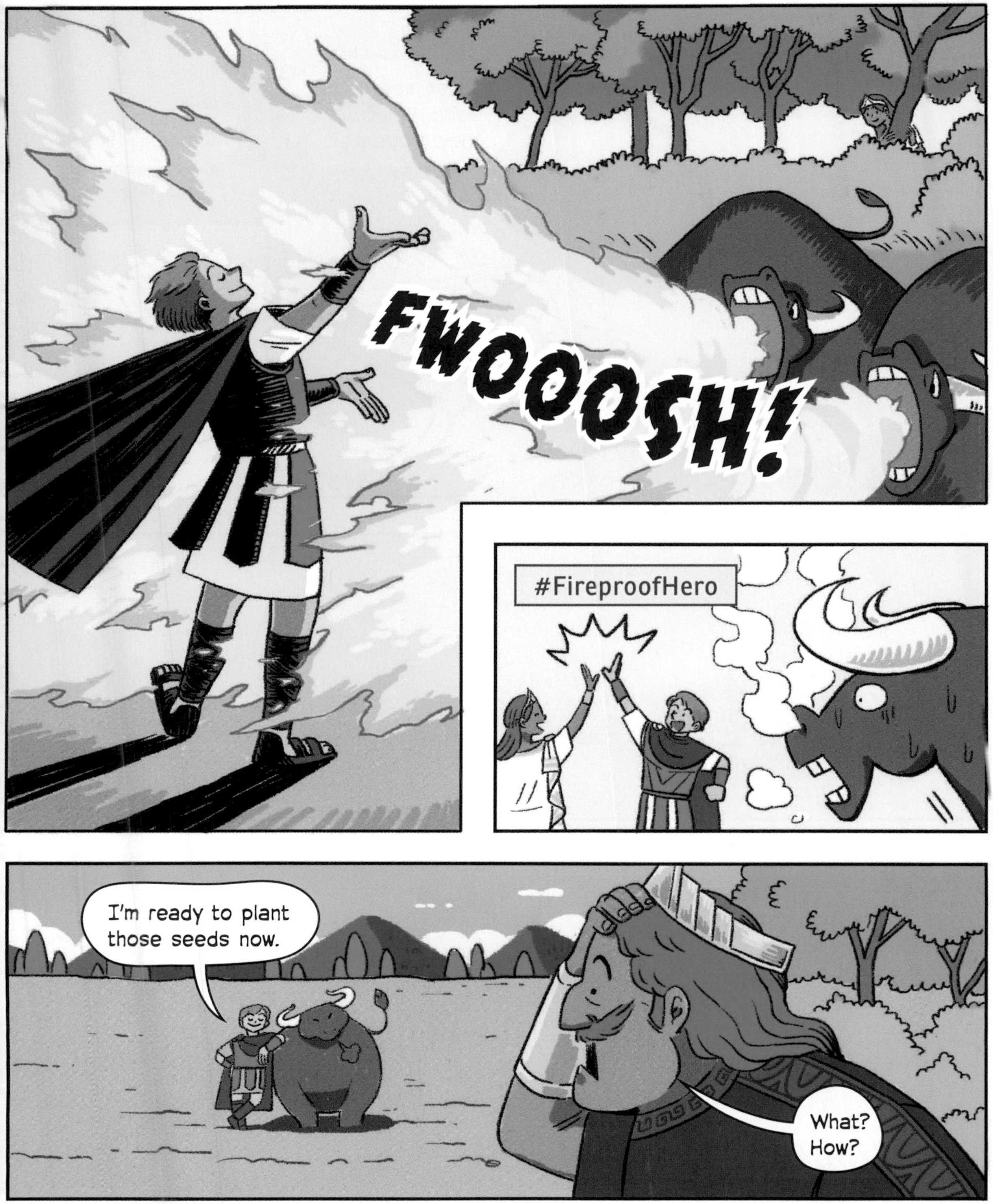
FWOOOSH!
#FireproofHero
I'm ready to plant those seeds now.
What? How?

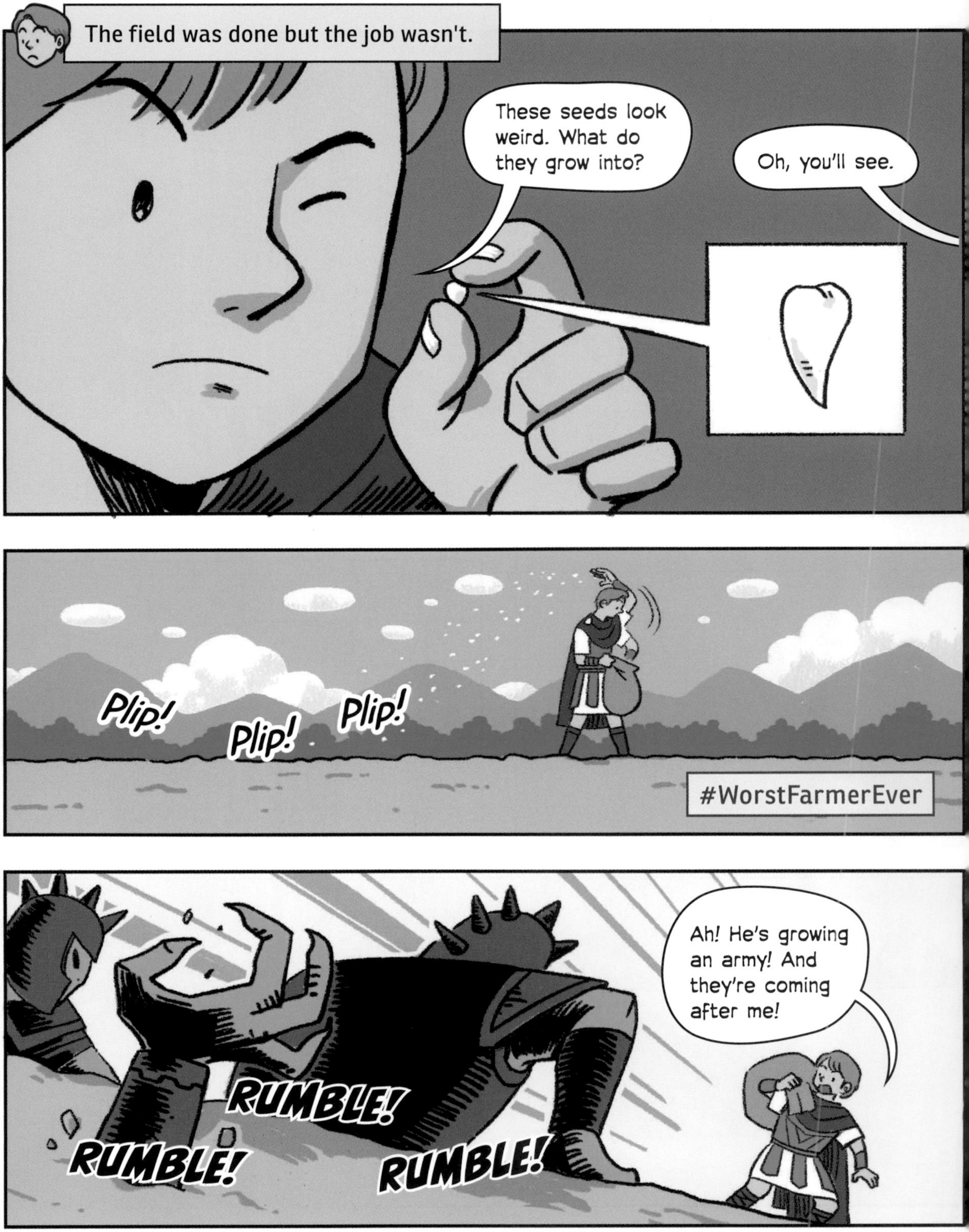
The field was done but the job wasn't.
These seeds look weird. What do they grow into?
Oh, you'll see.
Plip!
Plip!
Plip!
#WorstFarmerEver
RUMBLE!
RUMBLE!
RUMBLE!
Ah! He's growing an army! And they're coming after me!

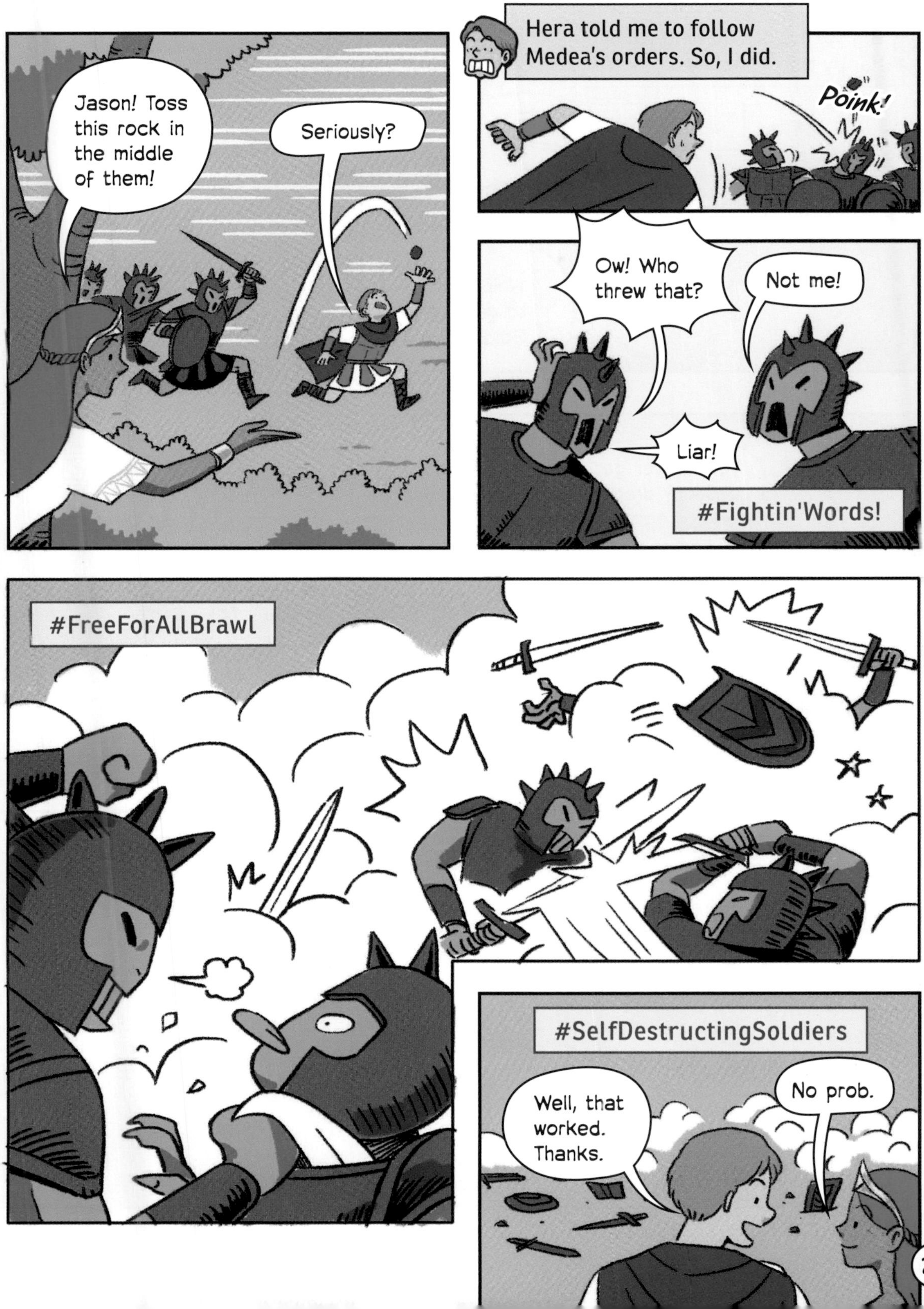
Jason! Toss this rock in the middle of them!
Seriously?
Hera told me to follow Medea's orders. So, I did.
Poink!
Ow! Who threw that?
Not me!
Liar!
#Fightin'Words!
#FreeForAllBrawl
#SelfDestructingSoldiers
Well, that worked. Thanks.
No prob.

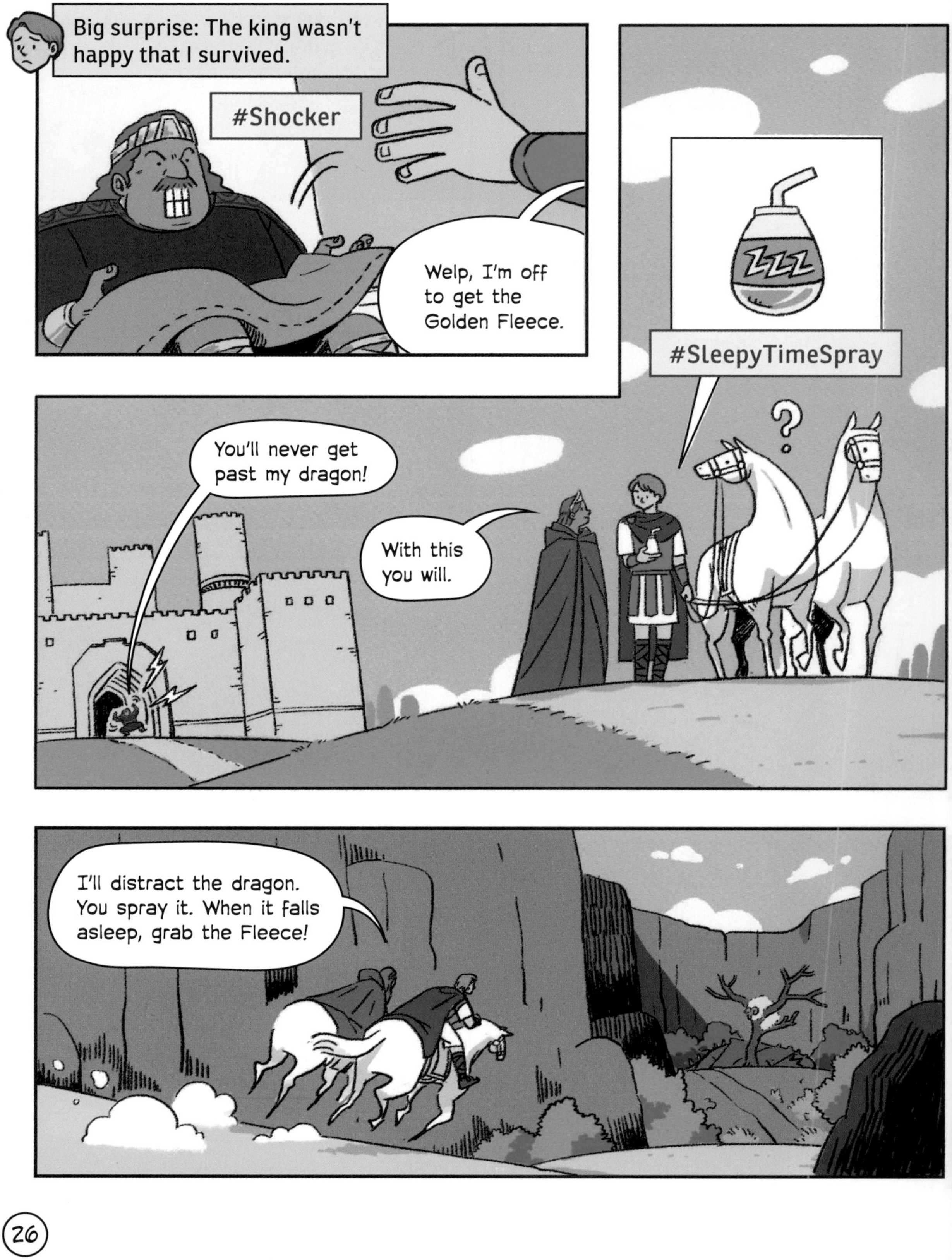
Big surprise: The king wasn't happy that I survived.
#Shocker
Welp, I'm off to get the Golden Fleece.
ZZZ
#SleepyTimeSpray
You'll never get past my dragon!
With this you will.
I'll distract the dragon. You spray it. When it falls asleep, grab the Fleece!

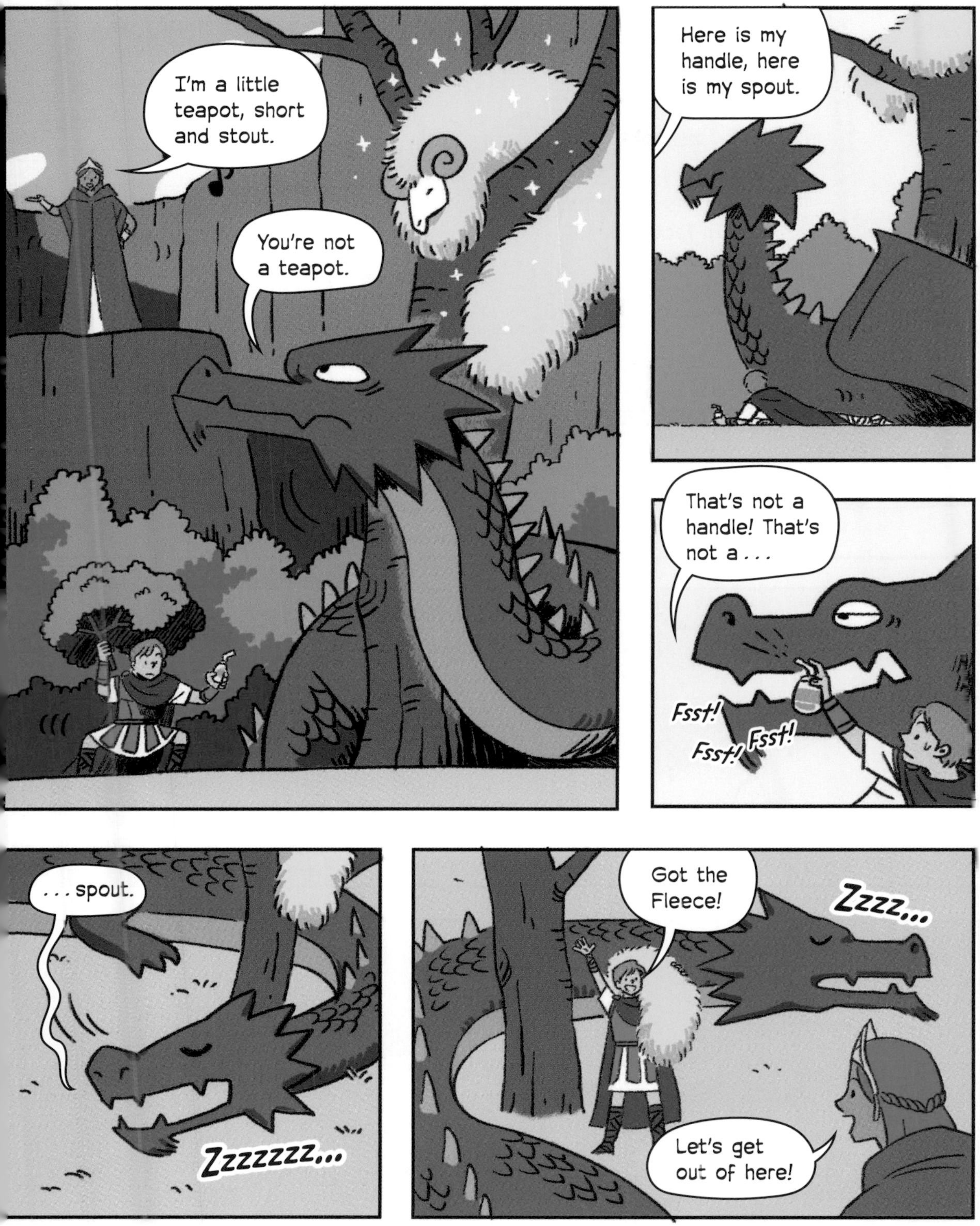
I'm a little teapot, short and stout.
You're not a teapot.
Here is my handle, here is my spout.
That's not a handle! That's not a . . .
Fsst!
Fsst!
Fsst!
. . . spout.
Zzzzzzz...
Got the Fleece!
Zzzz...
Let's get out of here!

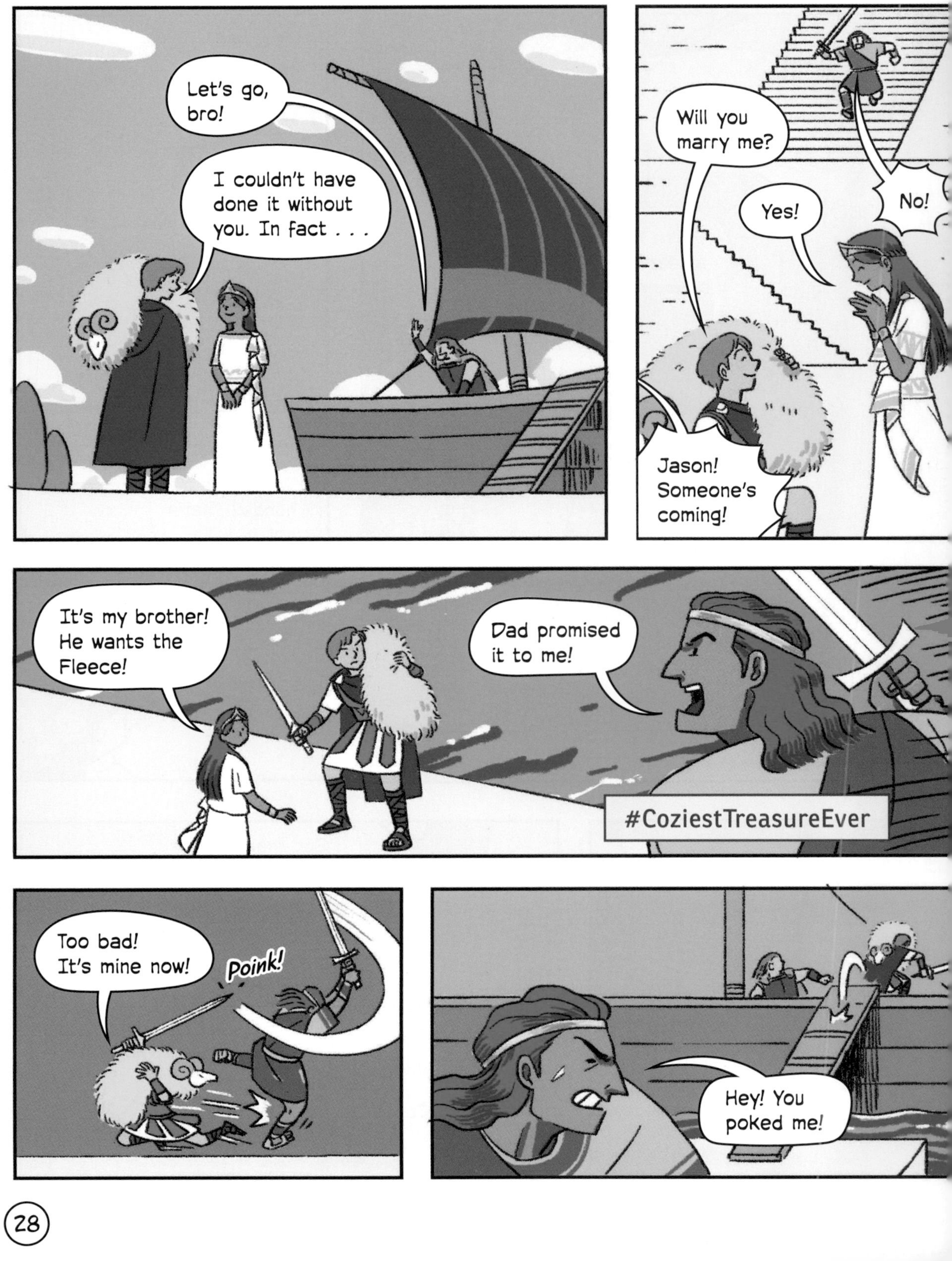
Let's go, bro!
I couldn't have done it without you. In fact . . .
Will you marry me?
Yes!
No!
Jason! Someone's coming!
It's my brother! He wants the Fleece!
Dad promised it to me!
#CoziestTreasureEver
Too bad! It's mine now!
Poink!
Hey! You poked me!

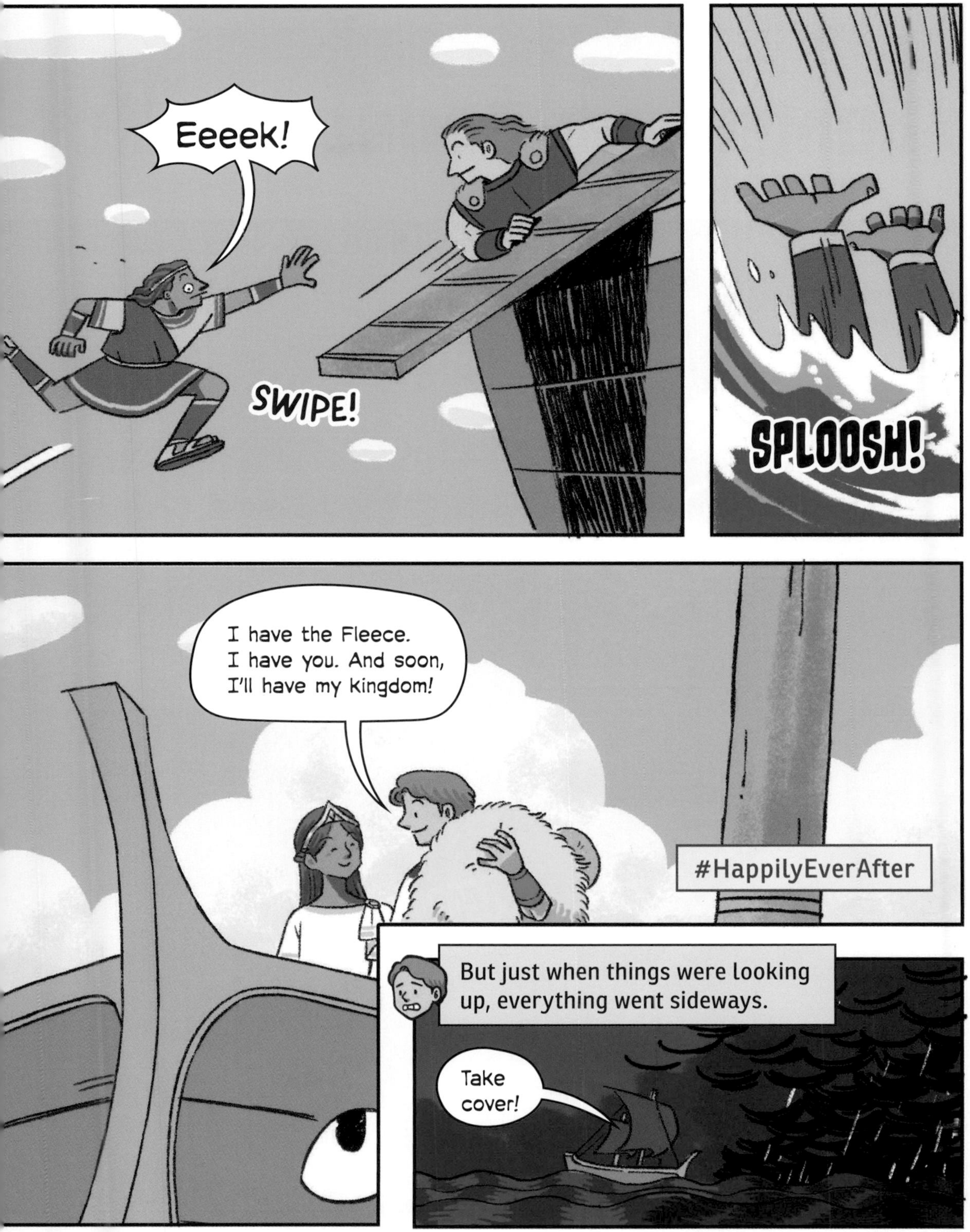
Eeeek!
SWIPE!
SPLOOSH!
I have the Fleece. I have you. And soon, I'll have my kingdom!
#HappilyEverAfter
But just when things were looking up, everything went sideways.
Take cover!

CHAPTER 4

HOMEWARD BOUND—OR NOT

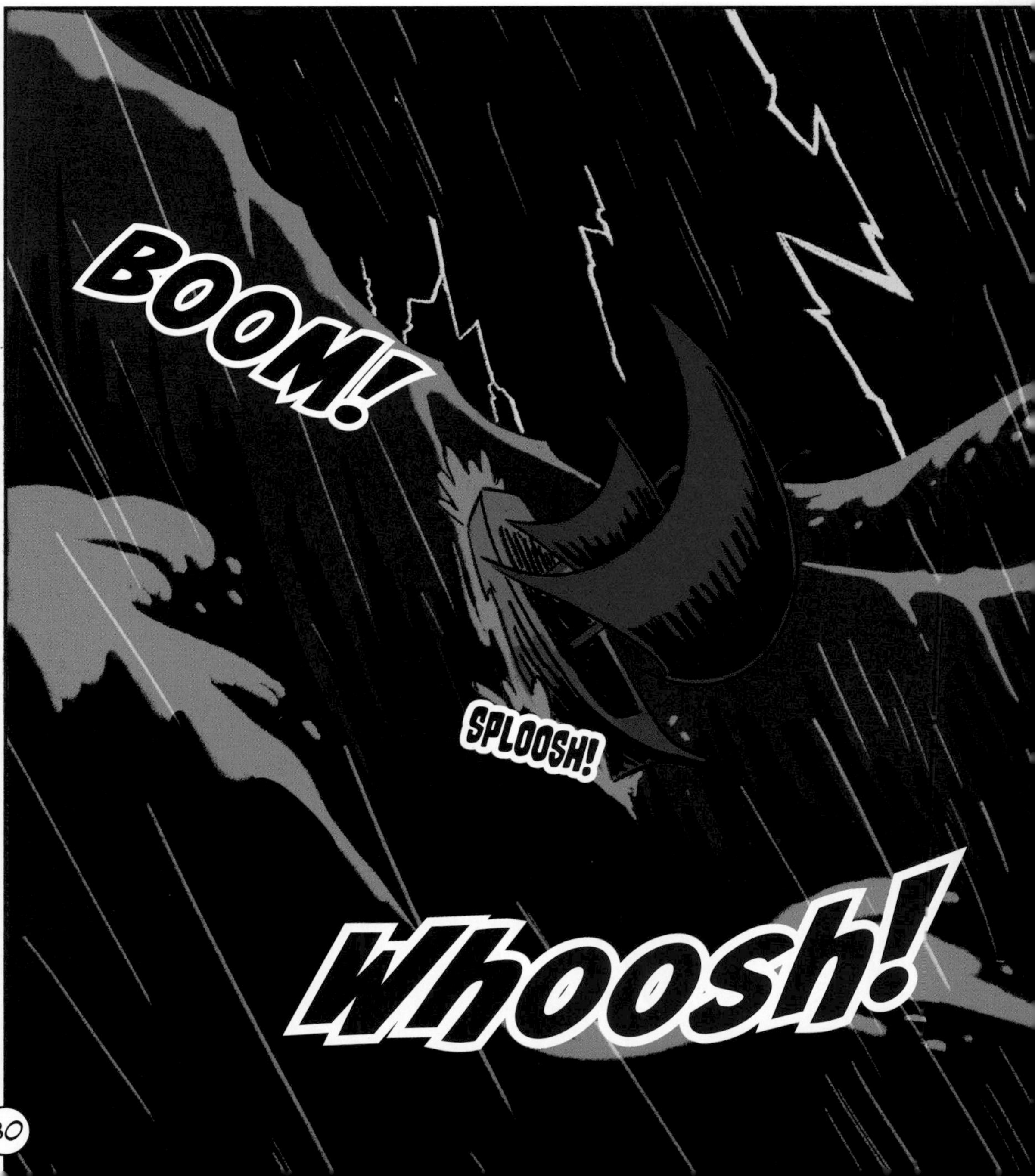
BOOOM!
SPLOOSH!
Whoosh!

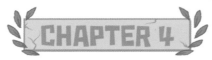

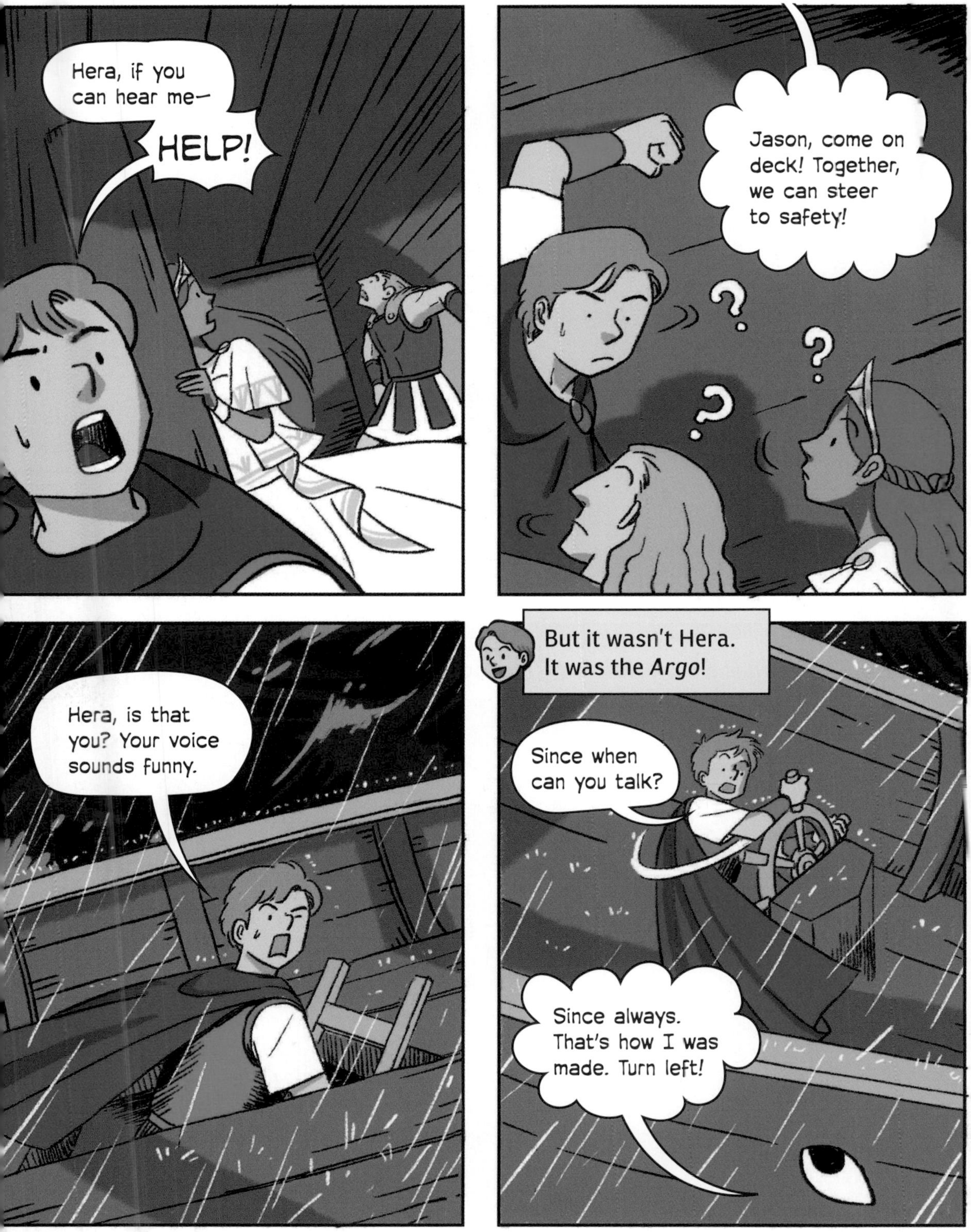
Hera, if you can hear me—
HELP!
Jason, come on deck! Together, we can steer to safety!
?
?
?
Hera, is that you? Your voice sounds funny.
But it wasn't Hera. It was the *Argo*!
Since when can you talk?
Since always. That's how I was made. Turn left!

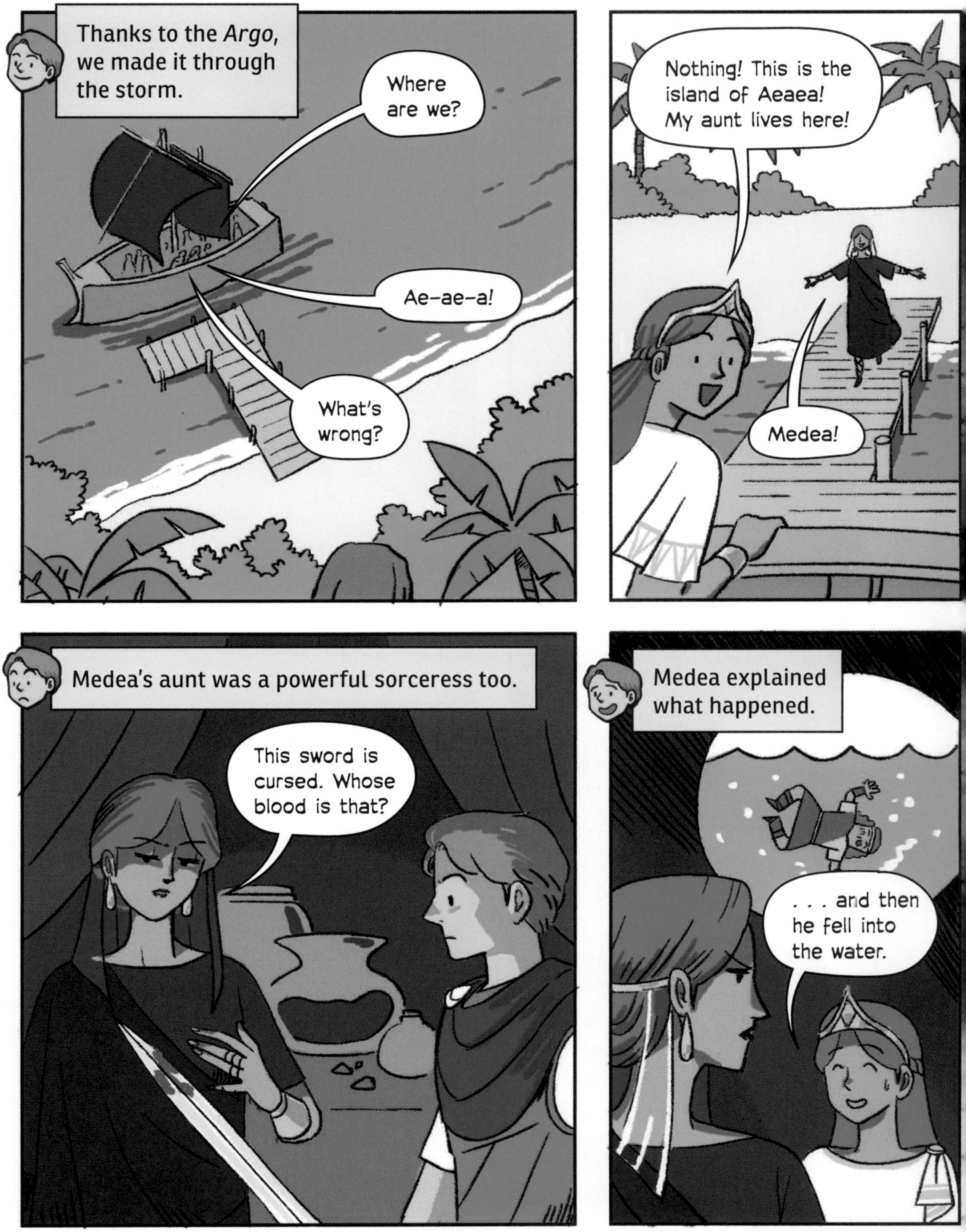
Thanks to the *Argo*, we made it through the storm.
Where are we?
Ae-ae-a!
What's wrong?
Nothing! This is the island of Aeaea! My aunt lives here!
Medea!
Medea's aunt was a powerful sorceress too.
This sword is cursed. Whose blood is that?
Medea explained what happened.
. . . and then he fell into the water.

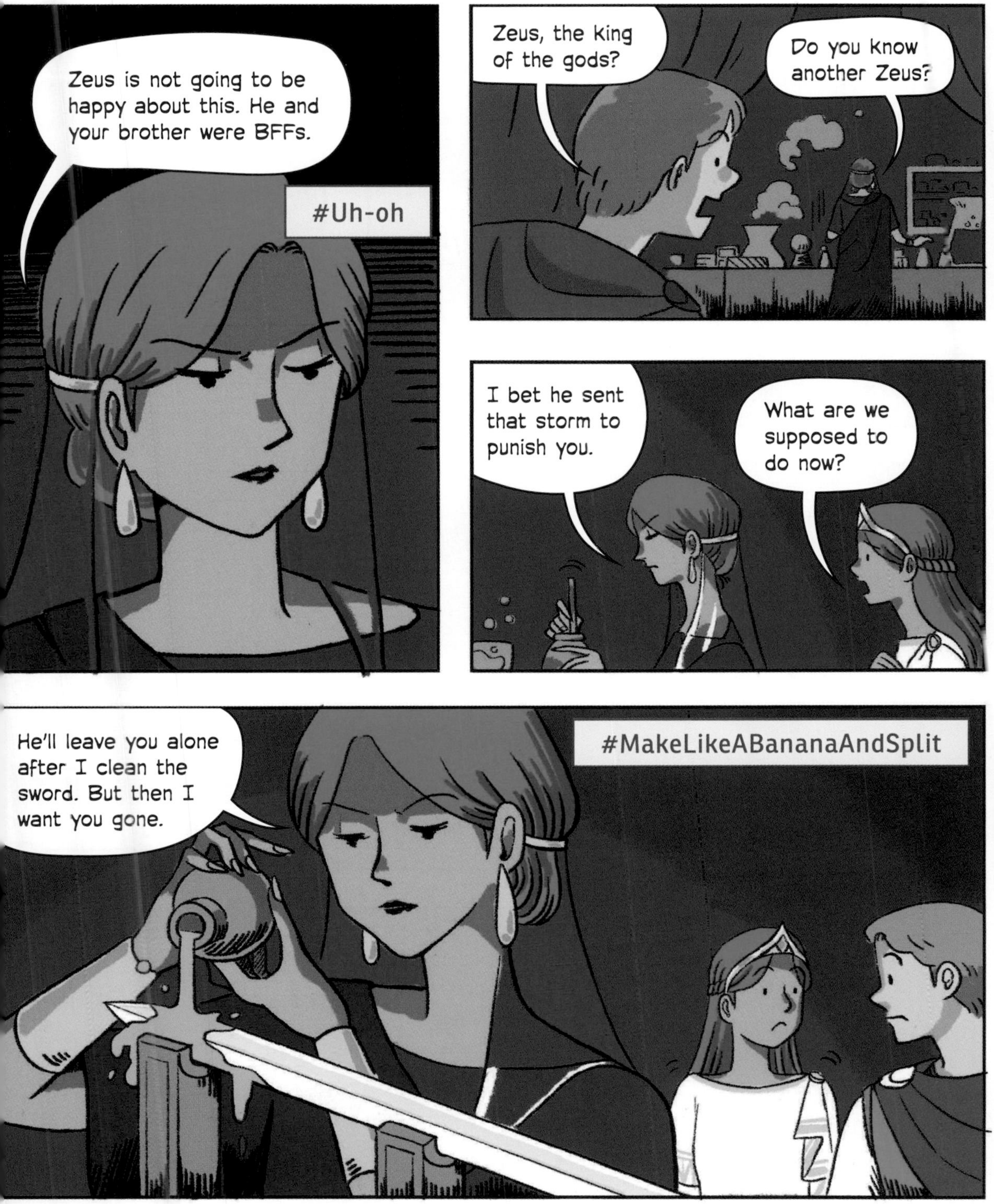
Zeus is not going to be happy about this. He and your brother were BFFs.
#Uh-oh
Zeus, the king of the gods?
Do you know another Zeus?
I bet he sent that storm to punish you.
What are we supposed to do now?
He'll leave you alone after I clean the sword. But then I want you gone.
#MakeLikeABananaAndSplit

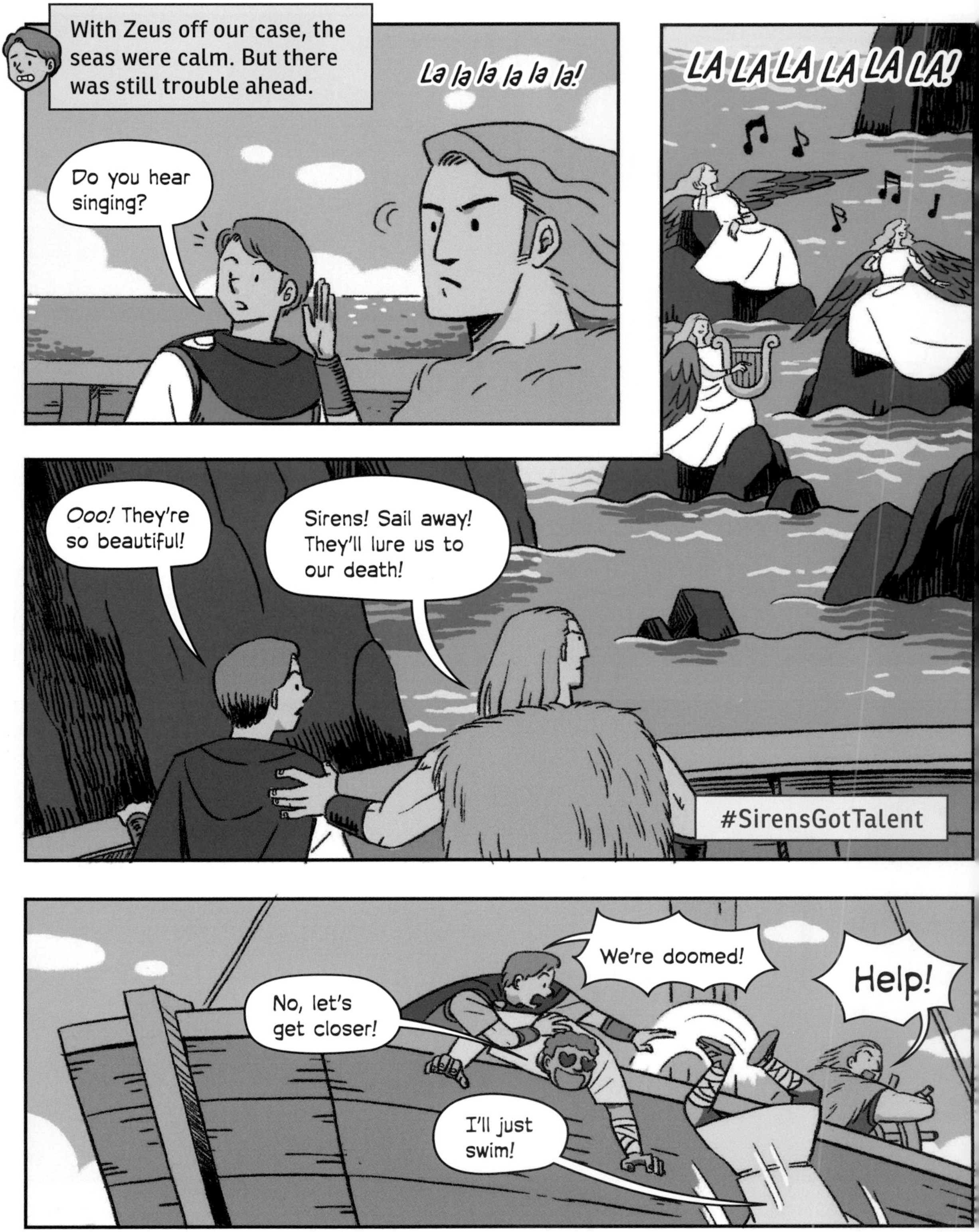
With Zeus off our case, the seas were calm. But there was still trouble ahead.
La la la la la la!
Do you hear singing?
LA LA LA LA LA LA!
Ooo! They're so beautiful!
Sirens! Sail away! They'll lure us to our death!
#SirensGotTalent
No, let's get closer!
We're doomed!
Help!
I'll just swim!

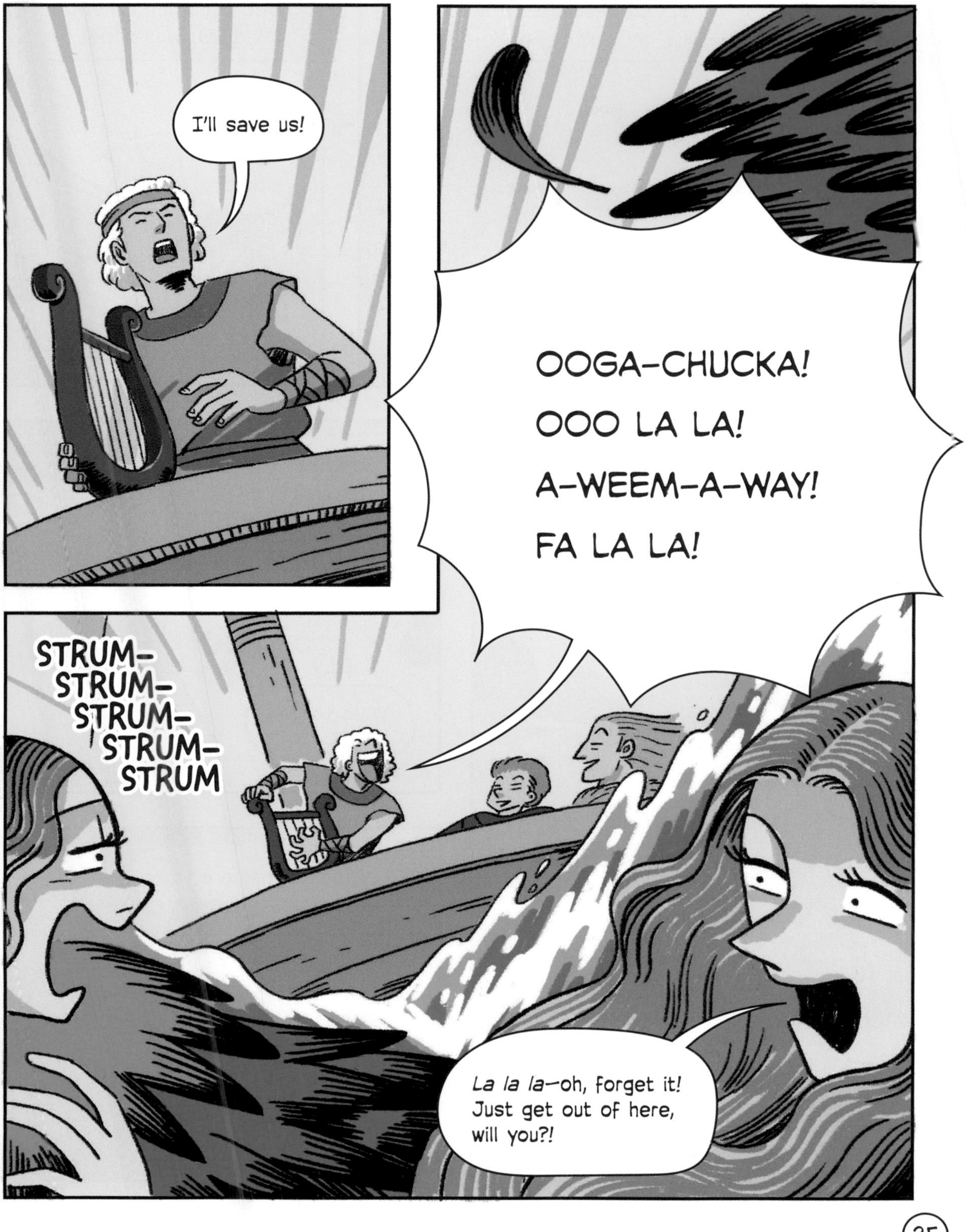
I'll save us!
OOGA-CHUCKA!
OOO LA LA!
A-WEEM-A-WAY!
FA LA LA!
STRUM-STRUM-STRUM-STRUM-STRUM
La la la—oh, forget it! Just get out of here, will you?!

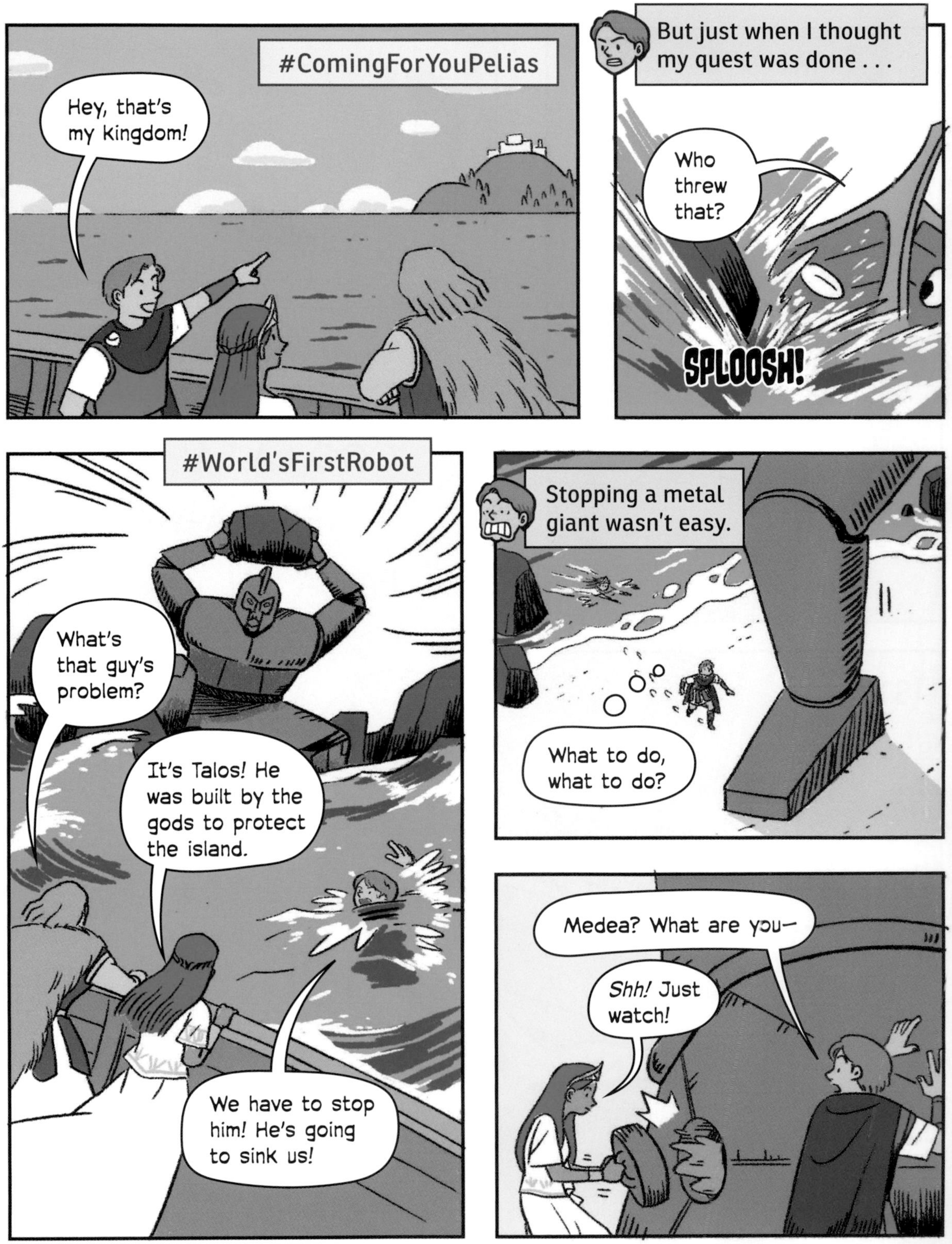
#ComingForYouPelias
Hey, that's my kingdom!
But just when I thought my quest was done . . .
Who threw that?
SPLOOSH!
#World'sFirstRobot
What's that guy's problem?
It's Talos! He was built by the gods to protect the island.
We have to stop him! He's going to sink us!
Stopping a metal giant wasn't easy.
What to do, what to do?
Medea? What are you—
Shh! Just watch!

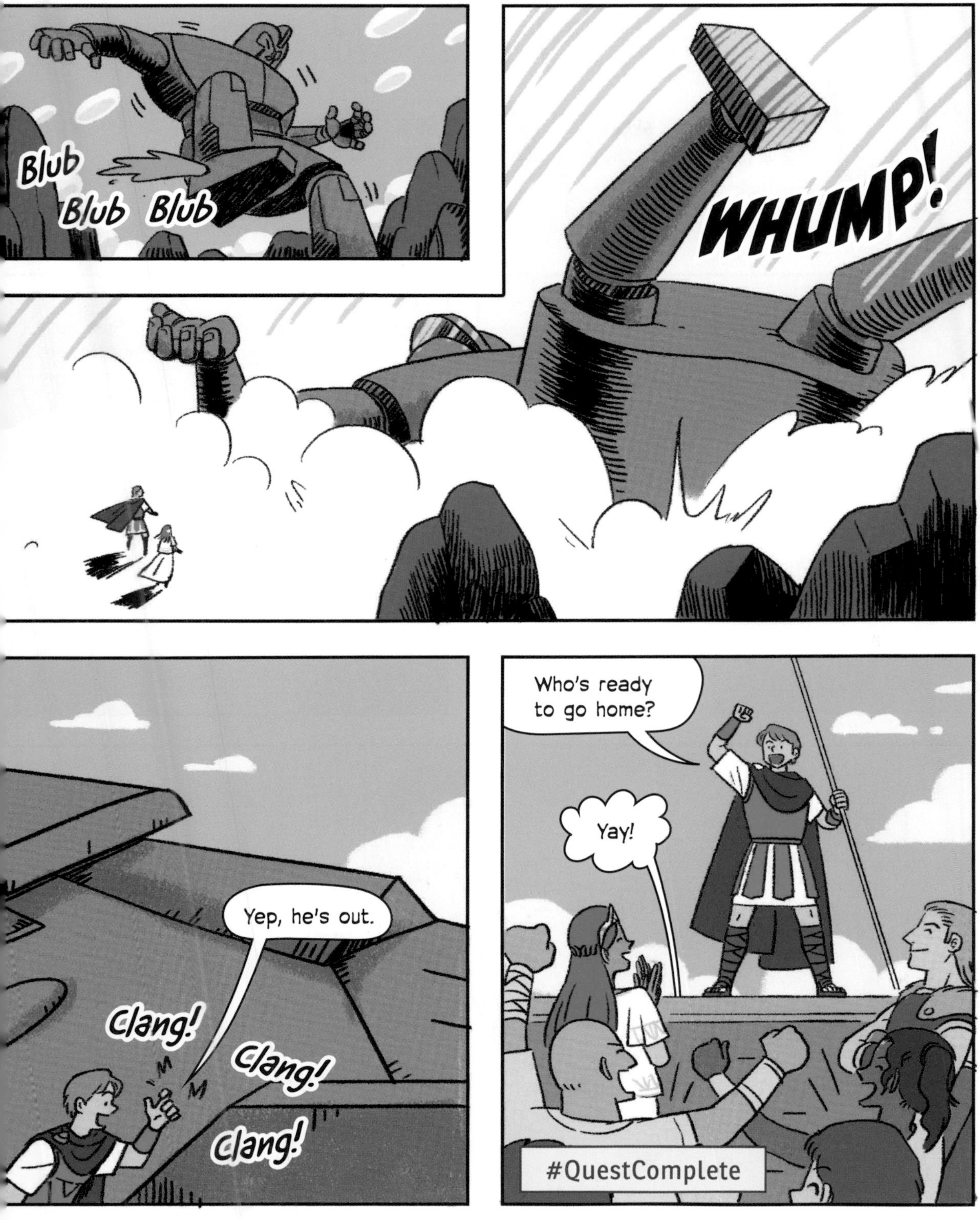
Blub
Blub Blub
WHUMP!
Yep, he's out.
Clang!
Clang!
Clang!
Who's ready to go home?
Yay!
#QuestComplete

CHAPTER 5

HAPPILY EVER AFTER?

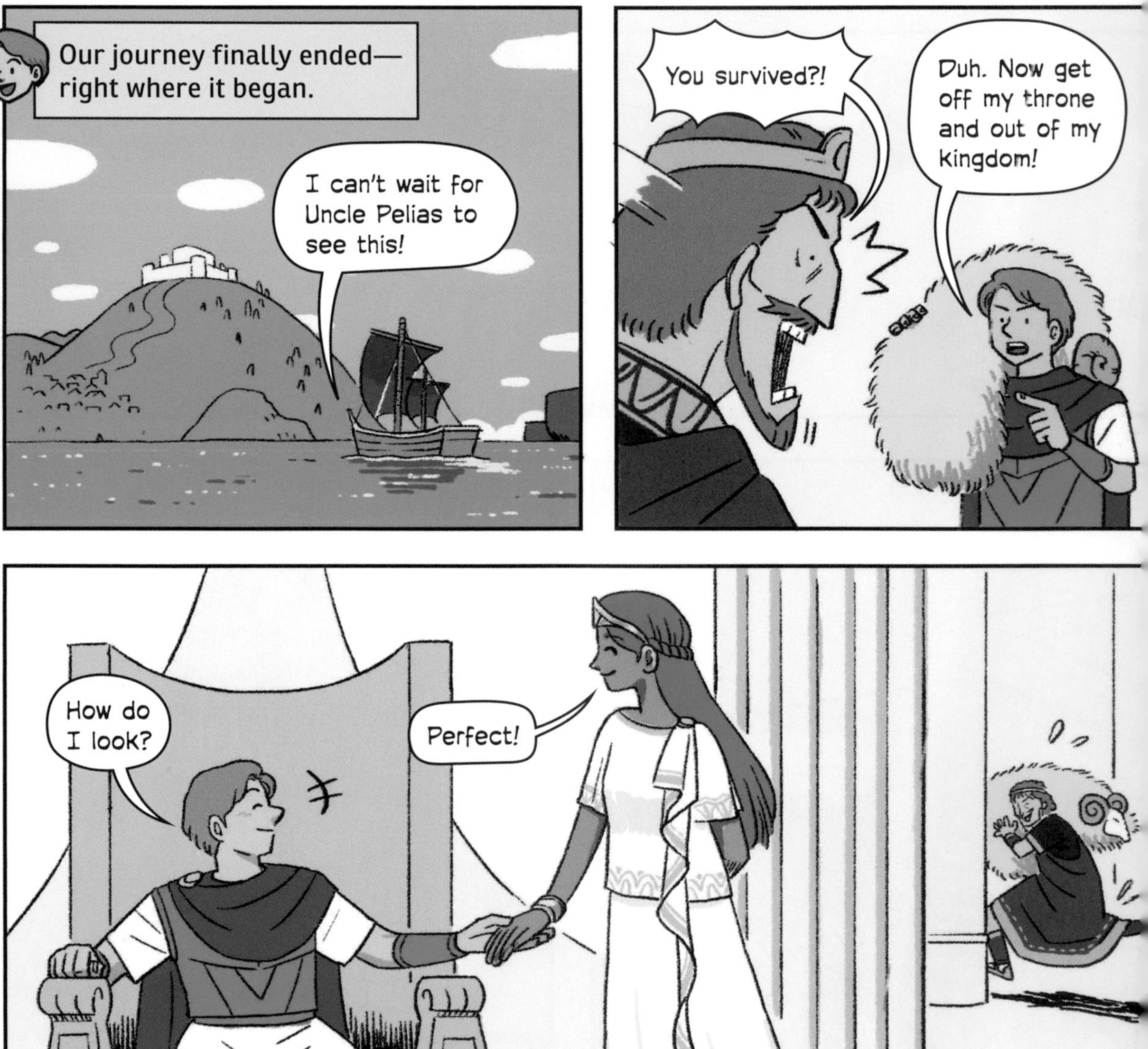
Our journey finally ended—right where it began.
I can't wait for Uncle Pelias to see this!
You survived?!
Duh. Now get off my throne and out of my kingdom!
How do I look?
Perfect!

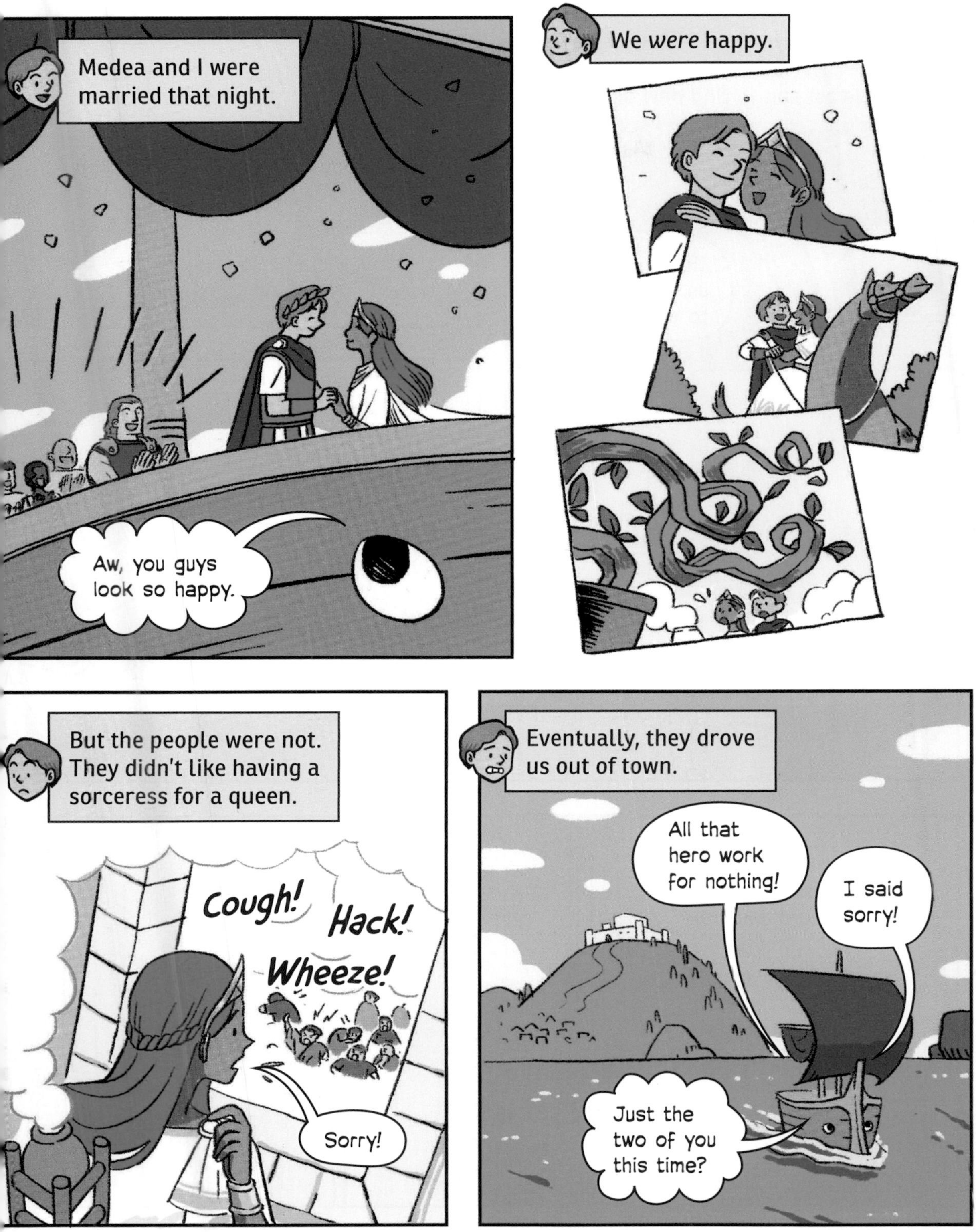
Medea and I were married that night.
Aw, you guys look so happy.
We *were* happy.
But the people were not. They didn't like having a sorceress for a queen.
Cough!
Hack!
Wheeze!
Sorry!
Eventually, they drove us out of town.
All that hero work for nothing!
I said sorry!
Just the two of you this time?

We set sail to find new digs.

Who are you?

The king sent us. He wants to see you.

Not you. Just Jason.

No one separates me from my husband!

Fsst!

Jason! Welcome! I heard you lost your throne.

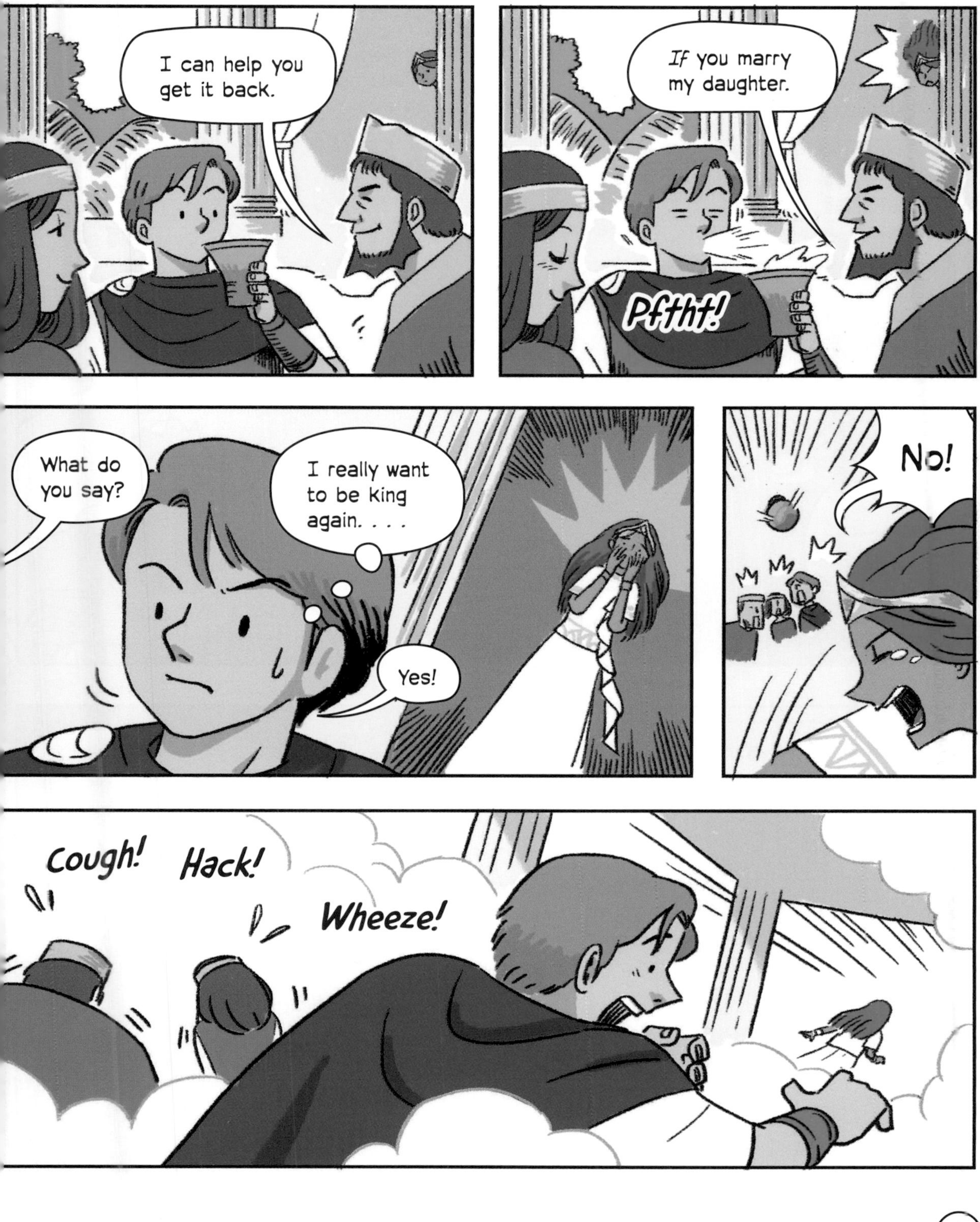
I can help you get it back.
If you marry my daughter.
Pftht!
What do you say?
I really want to be king again. . . .
Yes!
No!
Cough!
Hack!
Wheeze!

I woke up on the *Argo*.

Groan Where's Medea?

She flew off in a chariot pulled by dragons! I think she went to see Hera.

#EpicExit

If Hera finds out I planned to break up with Medea . . .

Just don't make her mad. Trust me, it's a bad idea to anger the gods!

Spoiler alert: Hera *did* find out.

How dare you? Medea is my friend!

Get us out of here, *Argo!*

On it!

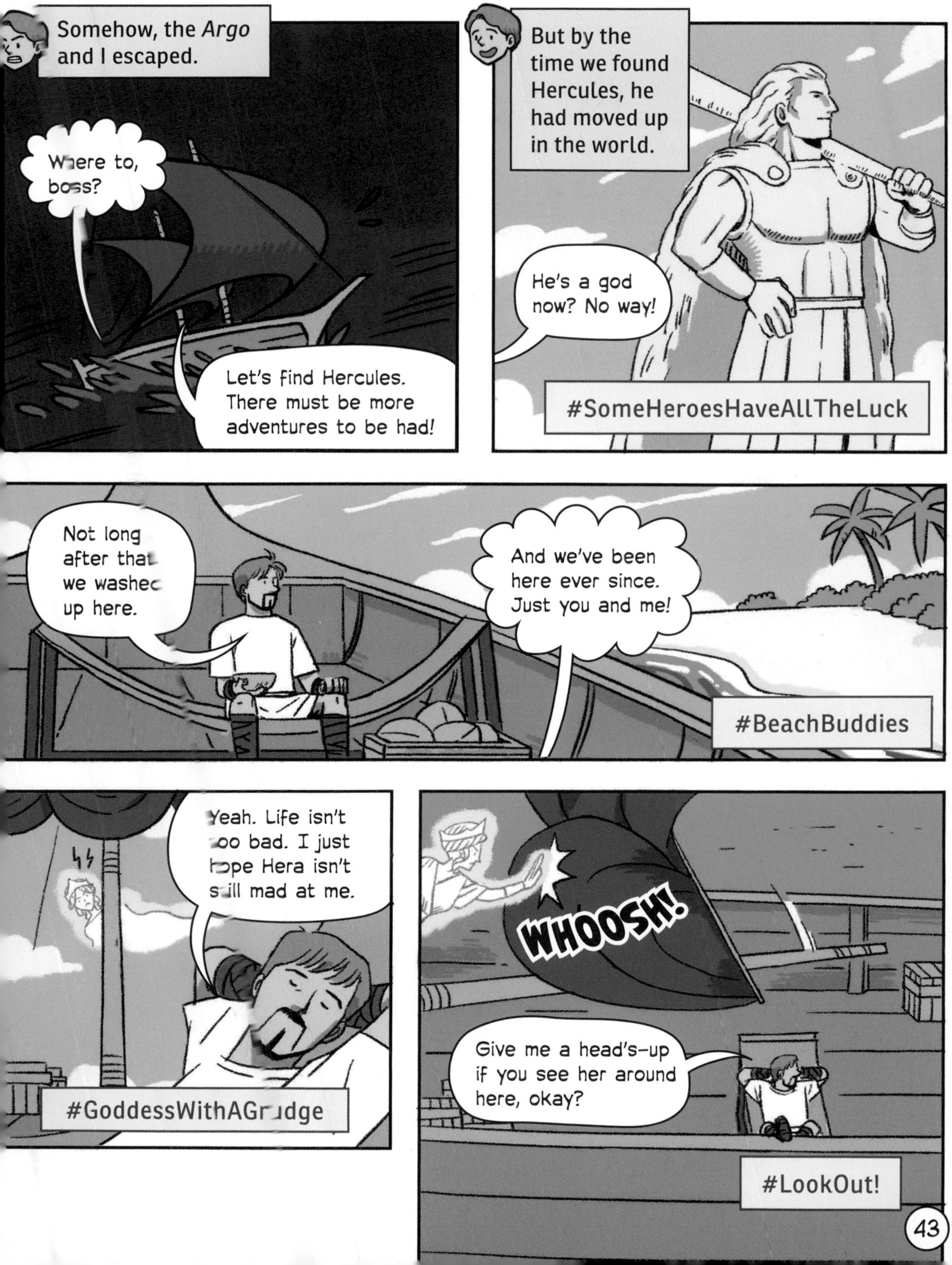
Somehow, the *Argo* and I escaped.
Where to, boss?
Let's find Hercules. There must be more adventures to be had!
But by the time we found Hercules, he had moved up in the world.
He's a god now? No way!
#SomeHeroesHaveAllTheLuck
Not long after that we washed up here.
And we've been here ever since. Just you and me!
#BeachBuddies
Yeah. Life isn't too bad. I just hope Hera isn't still mad at me.
#GoddessWithAGrudge
WHOOSH!
Give me a head's-up if you see her around here, okay?
#LookOut!

MORE ABOUT JASON AND THE ARGONAUTS

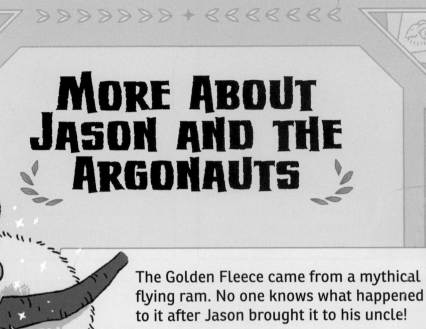

The Golden Fleece came from a mythical flying ram. No one knows what happened to it after Jason brought it to his uncle!

The Clashing Rocks slammed together so hard after the *Argo* sailed through that they never separated again.

The Argonaut who saved his fellow sailors from the Sirens was the hero Orpheus. He was a legendary Greek hero known for having the world's greatest musical skills.

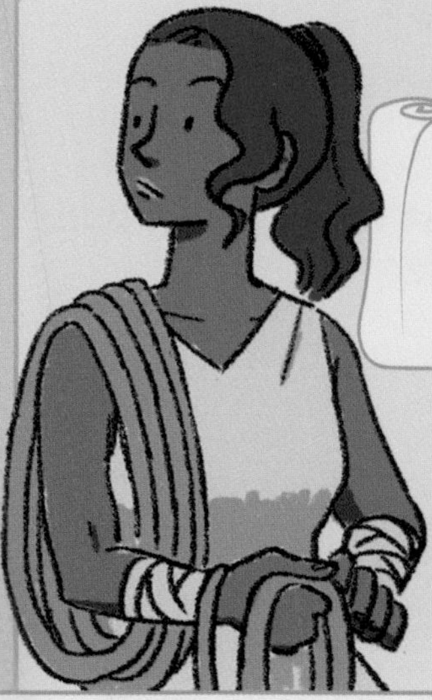

The only woman on board the *Argo* was the heroine Atalanta. She was known for her strength, cunning, and swiftness.

Jason discovered his father was still alive after all. He was just really old. Medea's magic reversed the aging process.

Medea is the granddaughter of Helios, the sun god. She used his chariot to fly away after Jason abandoned her.

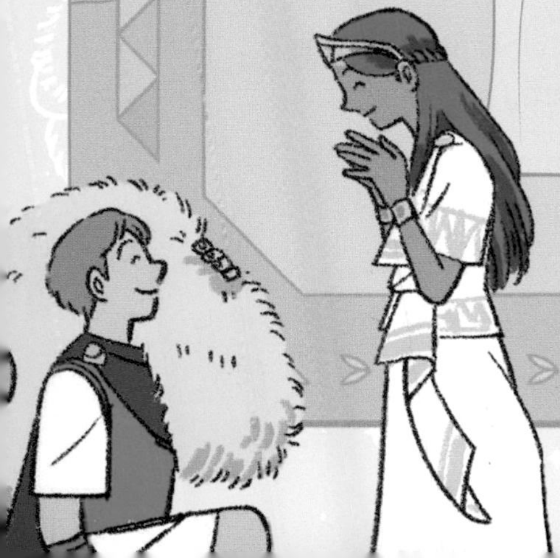

GLOSSARY

Argonaut (AR-go-not)—the name given to the sailors of the *Argo*

centaur (SEN-tohr)—mythical creature with the head and torso of a man and the body of a horse

chariot (CHAYR-ee-uht)—an ancient two-wheeled cart usually pulled by horses

fleece (FLEES)—the woolly coat of a sheep or ram

grudge (GRUHJ)—a strong lasting feeling of resentment toward someone for a real or imagined wrong

harpy (HAR-pee)—a mythical creature with the head of a woman and the body of a large bird

lure (LOOR)—to tempt or lead somewhere by offering some pleasure or advantage

quest (KWEST)—an adventurous journey

route (ROUT)—the path followed to get somewhere

sacred (SAY-krid)—dedicated or reserved for the worship of a god

Sirens (SY-rens)—a group of mythical women who lured sailors to their death by singing to them

sorceress (SOHR-ser-uhs)—a female magician who makes potions and casts spells and sometimes uses her power for evil

INTERNET SITES

Kiddle: Jason Facts for Kids
kids.kiddle.co/Jason

PBS: Jason & the Argonauts
pbs.org/mythsandheroes/myths_four_jason.html

The Argonauts: The Story of Jason and the Argonauts for Kids
theargonauts.com/the-story-of-jason-and-the-argonauts/

OTHER BOOKS IN THIS SERIES

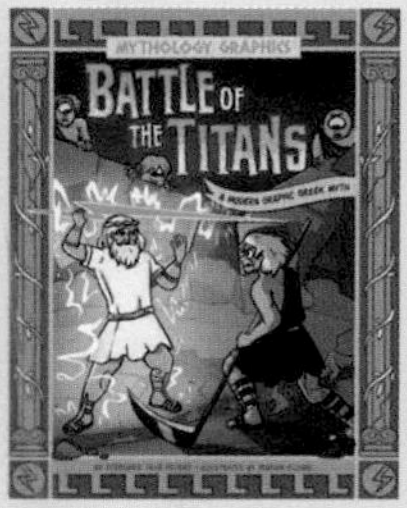
MYTHOLOGY GRAPHICS
BATTLE OF THE TITANS
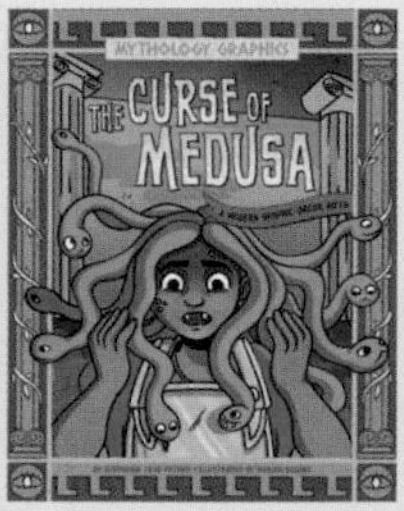
MYTHOLOGY GRAPHICS
THE CURSE OF MEDUSA
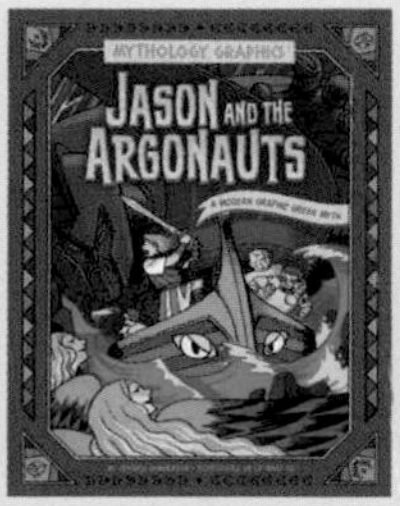
MYTHOLOGY GRAPHICS
JASON AND THE ARGONAUTS
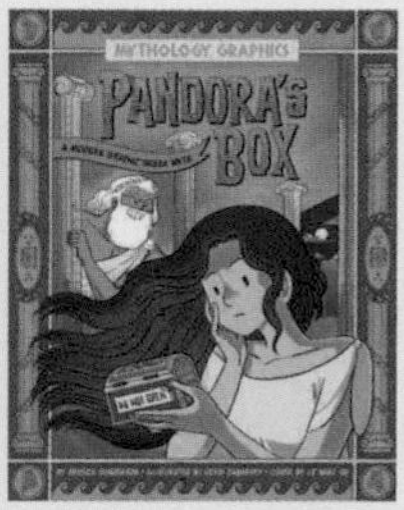
MYTHOLOGY GRAPHICS
PANDORA'S BOX
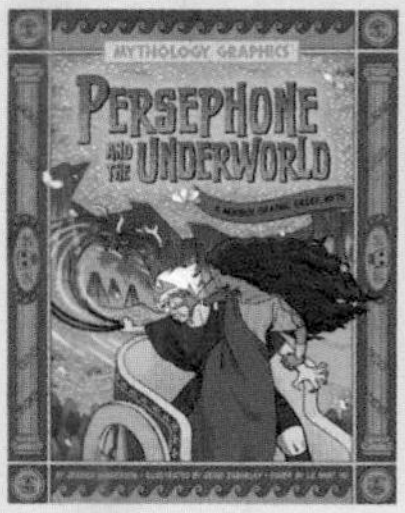
MYTHOLOGY GRAPHICS
PERSEPHONE AND THE UNDERWORLD
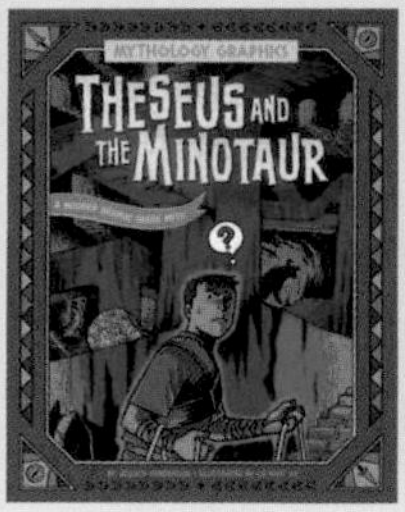
MYTHOLOGY GRAPHICS
THESEUS AND THE MINOTAUR
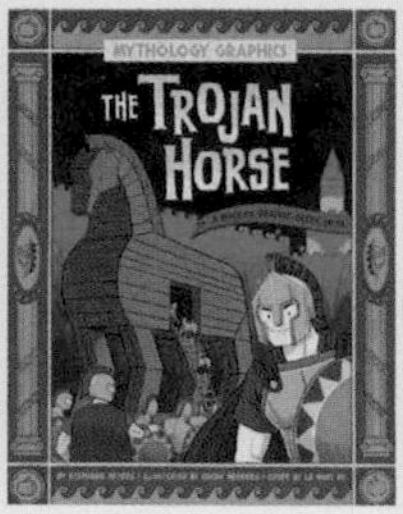
MYTHOLOGY GRAPHICS
THE TROJAN HORSE
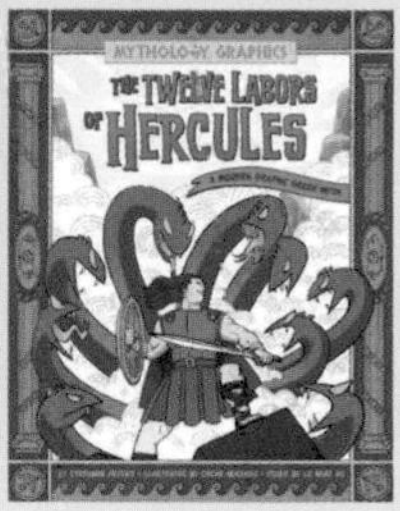
MYTHOLOGY GRAPHICS
THE TWELVE LABORS OF HERCULES

ABOUT THE CREATORS

Stephanie Peters has been writing books for children for more than 25 years. Her most recent Capstone titles include *The Unusual Journey from Pebbles to Continents: A Graphic Novel About Earth's Land*, as well as *The Twelve Labors of Hercules: A Modern Graphic Greek Myth* and *The Trojan Horse: A Modern Graphic Greek Myth* in the Mythology Graphics series. An avid reader, workout enthusiast, and beach wanderer, Stephanie enjoys spending time with her family and their pets. She lives and works in Mansfield, Massachusetts.

Le Nhat Vu was born in Nha Trang, a seaside city in Vietnam. He now works as a book illustrator in Ho Chi Minh City. He draws inspiration from fantasy, adventure, and poetic stories. During his free time, he enjoys reading Japanese comics (manga) and novels as well as watching football and movies—maybe with a cup of milk coffee.